NEW INTERIOR DESIGN
COLLIDOSCOPE

NIGEL COATES

NEW INTERIOR DESIGN
COLLIDOSCOPE

NIGEL COATES

LAURENCE KING PUBLISHING LTD
in association with
HARPER DESIGN INTERNATIONAL
an imprint of HarperCollins*Publishers*

LAURENCE KING

Published in 2004 by Laurence King Publishing Ltd.
71 Great Russell Street
London WC1B 3BP
United Kingdom
Tel: +44 20 7430 8850
Fax: +44 20 7430 8880
Email: enquiries@laurenceking.co.uk
www.laurenceking.co.uk

Published in North and South America by:
Harper Design International,
An imprint of HarperCollins*Publishers*
10 East 53rd Street
New York, NY 10022
Tel: (212) 207-7000
Fax: (212) 207-7654
HarperDesign@harpercollins.com
www.harpercollins.com

Text copyright © 2004 Nigel Coates
This book was designed and produced by Laurence King Publishing Ltd.

Library of Congress Control Number: 2004111919

ISBN 1 85669 388 0

Design by **BARK**: www.barkdesign.net
Picture research by Jennifer Hudson

Printed in China

contents

Introduction

What does the word 'interior' mean in this day and age? Beyond the cusp of the millennium, finally we are witnessing a gradual breakdown of professional roles and, as for all other cultural forms, that means that the interior often breaks through walls. We can talk about outdoor interiors, or public spaces as living rooms and, at the other end of the scale, about the interior of the mind. The big question that this book asks is how these opposites affect one another. By starting from a series of generic containers, *Collidoscope* explores a spread of possibilities, and the interplay between approaches.

By approaches I am careful not to mean styles. My own interest is to interrogate design from the point of view of the intention of the designer, and the mode through which a room communicates. To look at design as a series of set styles is less interesting than looking at the crossovers, hence the notion of collision that can work against the organizing principle of the lexicon. The whole point of spatial design is for it to generate animated meanings that can correspond to your demand for elaborate functional possibilities. Gone are the days when you could only wash in the bathroom or eat in the dining room; interiors now are about states of becoming.

We live in interiors of many sorts – not just those we choose to call home, but those we visit in our own and in other cities. Influences spring out at us from the most unexpected places, yet these may not necessarily have been touched by designers. It could be a shack on the beach, a workers' café, a ruin or a railway station. That is not to undervalue the skills that professional designers can impart, many eloquent examples of which are included here, but the value of the interior is as much in the eye of the beholder as in that of the designer. All those make-over TV shows are proof that everyone wants to have a go.

Many architects and designers have shifted their fields of practice away from making the entirely new to adjusting what is already there. Any architect worth his salt ought to be able to do an inside too. Space is as often recycled as built from scratch, which has become a phenomenon that interests architects (and even some clients) from an intellectual standpoint. Almost none of the imaginative force that architects can offer is channelled into new buildings compared to the effort that goes into changing existing ones.

Some shop owners have even gone so far with this that they are opening stores on a deliberately temporary basis. Comme des Garçons and other ultra-stylish labels are experimenting with the charity shop, move-in-over-the-weekend approach. By doing so, they are undercutting the assumption that high-priced clothes means piled-on design, and are asserting that some of the hippest places in town are spontaneous. The occupant can be the designer by making the most of the misfit between the space and its function.

So this book is built on a simple idea – to reflect the kaleidoscopic world we live in, to activate the intrusions that are part of modern life. The principle of merely selecting a style is as outdated as pigeon post. What we do more is endlessly reinterpret functions and references. We can play with what a space does not need to be. We can make it connect on many levels, and capitalize on the designer's instinct to make a space unique by playing it off others.

Almost all the designers here are making use of the situation they are designing and how this plays against the city that surrounds it. Whether in New York or Tokyo, Barcelona or Berlin, we are witnessing the practice of design in an ever-shifting collage of global experiences. We constantly field the subtle balance between connection and disconnection, and the interiors here all make some attempt to map out moods and actions. *Collidoscope* is a kit of parts, a spectrum, a loose form of classification that instantly declassifies. It is not absolute, but reflects the interests and methods of our time. In crossing references, it encourages a diffuse view of the world and of what it can provide to make places that do not yet exist. It suggests a continual rotation of influences that may pop up where they are least expected.

But like all systems of cross-reference, here I have devised a straightforward taxonomy that provides a framework of groupings that beg reconfiguration. This circular set of containers, such as Bodies, Nests and Movies, sets a process in motion and maps out a series of 'homes' that can draw together a diverse collection of interiors indicative of our time. Rather than reading too much into the divisions, think of what lies between them, how they could collide and infect one another. Crossover and collision help define this book, and indicate a process that you, the reader, can finish by imagining the next steps in this process.

Tokyo's urban landscape seems to thrive on an interminable riot of experiments designed to outdo each other. Though originally fired by a desire to import all things modern, the city's success at ersatz reproduction seems to have eclipsed its origins, or at least to have learnt to sustain itself. Areas like Shibuya and Roppongi became hives of every possible cast of fashionable lifestyle, encapsulated in independent but complete worlds. There would be a Rasta café on the eleventh floor, next to a karaoke bar next to a noodle shop. No map or conventional guide could reveal all.

Whether in Tokyo, Madrid, Vancouver or London, the sheer intensity of the lifestyle hives we inhabit means each of us urbanites builds a quite separate map in our mind, and that the city is experienced as a vast pinball machine of urban events. The brightest destinations will always hope to outdo the others, but for many that will be the very reason to avoid them. We are all different and that's what we should expect to find in the vast array of options we have open to us wherever we are. And that travel is as important as the image. Here, in *Collidoscope*, I hope you find yourself in a global net of rooms that will add to your already vast experience of interiors, and that this book will sit happily on your shelves and, at least for a while, be part of the room you live in.

Ichthus' dynamic interiors are a powerful antidote to the featureless 1970s complex in which they are located. Luminous walls covered in distorted digital imagery define the classroom spaces, while a basket-weave construction of plywood ribs and beech strips (containing three meeting rooms) snakes through the central space.

ARCHITECT: **24H ARCHITECTURE**   PROJECT: **ICHTHUS BUSINESS CENTRE, ROTTERDAM**

BODIES

No interior would be worth its salt if it did not have room for bodies: your body, my body, their bodies. Interiors have always configured the social spaces we constantly form and re-form. But body awareness has never been greater. The body is central to the cultural foreground, so it follows that it must be part of the contemporary language of the interior. Bodies can be represented by interiors and in them. Consciously doing so by design is a way of reinforcing a sense of belonging or, alternatively, of competing to occupy the same space.

The first time you turn up for lessons at the Ichthus Business Centre, you are in for a surprise. Forget about those rigid walled classrooms you knew at school. These learning spaces are all linked and flow into one another. The design of the centre makes a clever adaptation of a run-of-the mill office building by creating a world of interactivity. Views from the windows are filtered through translucent gauze, which shifts the focus to the inside, where the walls are punched with light or are covered with giant digital prints.

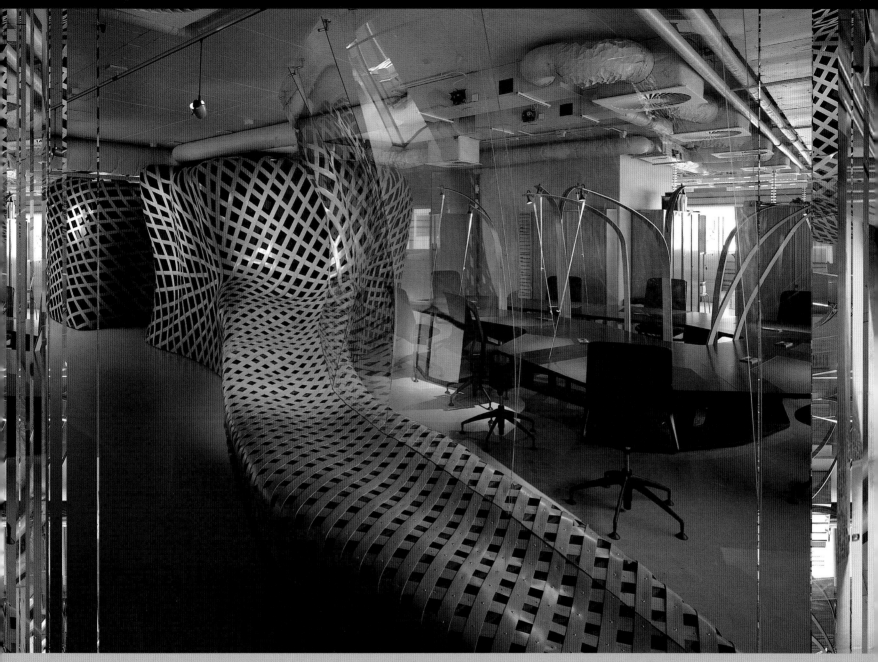

These treatments are organized by a series of ribbons that weave between the building's original grid of columns, sweeping into generous spaces where you can chat, relax or study. The whole is really held together by the hybrid structure at its core. This hub of the hive both occupies the centre of the building and holds all its disparate parts together, combining an interview room with the lobby area. It has been achieved with a basket-like structure that expands and contracts as it passes over the required bumps and curves needed to define the various spaces that it borders. At the centre of it, a tunnel passes right through; but, like a reclining figure, this structure distends at the outer extremities into a surface on which you can sit.

Although the whole project is full of contrasts of material and form, these are not simply butted but are overlapped. The designers have taken great pleasure in occasionally revealing the old building and, when they do, in diverting attention away from it. They have deliberately left parts such as the ducting and services system exposed as if to reveal the inner workings of the hive.

Some of the work areas extend this sense of alien occupation. Elongated and oversized tables have sinuous light fittings hanging over each work area. Though the spaces are predominantly open, details like these give you the impression that all is in motion, or that elements in them had grown that morning. However, it is the oversized body at the centre that remains the first occupant of the space and, as such, stands in for our own bodies, which come later. The design has contrasts of scale, texture and image to make a rich palette of sensation and meaning.

They add up to a complete world that encourages everyone inside to figure out how to make use of it themselves. As with any ideal learning environment, what it looks like is less important than how it feels when you use it.

Sportopia is a sadomasochistic playpen given to toning muscles for sexual pleasure. Van Lieshout's obsessions with the body – physical exertion, passion, ecstasy and finally relaxation – have produced an extreme sculpture cum leisure space. A mezzanine level is devoted almost entirely to a series of 30 connected beds designed for communal slumber.

DESIGNERS: **ATELIER VAN LIESHOUT**   PROJECT: **SPORTOPIA, SÃO PAULO BIENAL, 2002**

Sportopia by the Atelier van Lieshout is similarly open-ended, but is also an autonomous structure. Built for the São Paulo Bienal of 2002, it was an unusually plausible art piece, a convincing but hypothetical collective inhabitation space. The key is its functional diversity, together with its absolute consistency of execution. Sportopia combines sport with sex, eating and sleeping, as though sport were a sufficiently cohesive concept to tie a whole society together. Its overriding metaphor is undoubtedly the human body, both in its consistency of construction and in terms of the user, the ways in which it provokes you to contort and interact on many different, often unimaginable levels.

Although any sitting room or home connects to the body image in various ways, Sportopia encapsulates the link between body awareness and the drive for pleasure in contemporary lifestyle culture. Its rawness and its multiple invitations to indulge in extreme behaviour mirror and expose the sheer invention that many of us put into the use of everyday environments in order to experience pleasure.

Unlike the European image of the whorehouse or dedicated sex space, and perhaps more like the rooms in some Japanese love hotels, it overtly allies convenience to the scenarios of hardcore leisure. Its materials might be steel, wood and concrete, but the currency of meaning centres on the body and the many gymnastic acts it can perform – and all the more ambiguously so when in a public arena like this one.

Made from a commonly available scaffolding system, the structure has a deliberate industrial harshness. It makes use of the attraction inherent in a rough interior. This rawness suggests exposure and, in turn, sexual frisson. The two-storey longitudinal structure is overtly functional and direct – spindly columns and cross-members define a framework on which a spectrum of activities can be performed. Its improvised character, its smell, its sweat, invite transgression.

The lower level is kitted out with a series of benches set up for exercise, with crude dumb-bells and concrete weights. One bench looks more like a gynaecologist's chair. Any strict regime

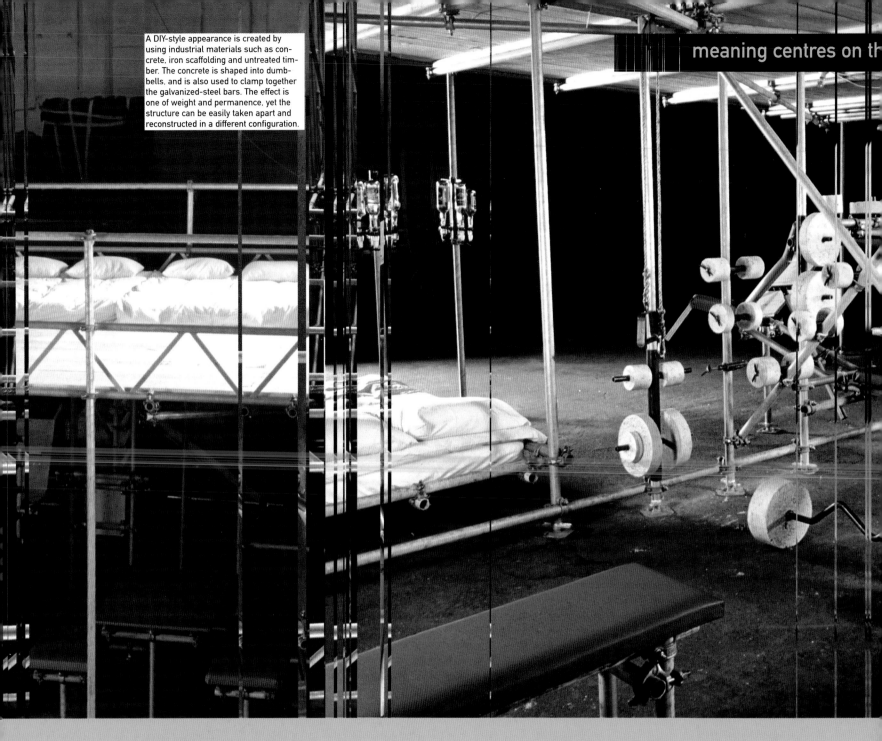

A DIY-style appearance is created by using industrial materials such as concrete, iron scaffolding and untreated timber. The concrete is shaped into dumbbells, and is also used to clamp together the galvanized-steel bars. The effect is one of weight and permanence, yet the structure can be easily taken apart and reconstructed in a different configuration.

of exercise is slightly undermined by the convenient spirit dispenser with upturned shot-bottles attached to one of the columns. One end incorporates a dining area, a cage (ambiguously a larder or sex den) and a kitchen.

The upstairs level of Sportopia is almost entirely taken up by a single, dormitory-style bed. After a healthy group session downstairs, the entire community can retire up there to enjoy a collective chill-out, followed by a wash and brush up in the wooden cabin at the end.

Although shown in an art context, the implications of Sportopia are about reconfiguring contemporary urban lifestyle and the way architecture facilitates it. This is not a building, but a structure within a building – both an interior and an entire world. It celebrates the fact that it has no contact with outside influence, apart from human nature.

It signifies both the body in a room and a building on its own. And this is substantiated by all the direct references to body culture and its hedonistic counterparts; although essentially not that

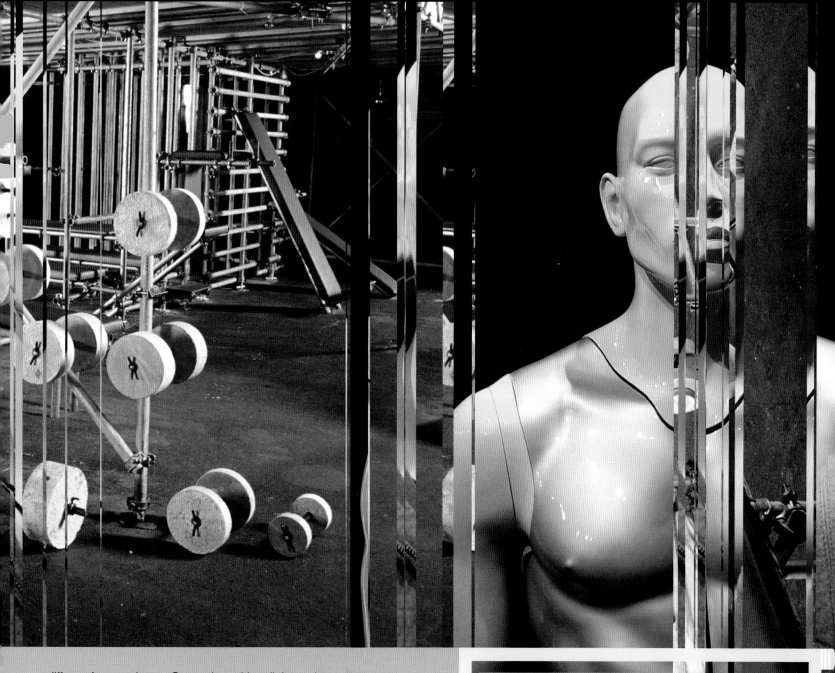

different from any house, Sportopia enables all these elements to be physically joined. The central 'spine' of the structure is the logical and structural core of what folds out from it. Lighting is a strange omission from this self-sufficient structure. We see it here as we do a sculpture in a gallery, with the object well lit within a field of relative darkness.

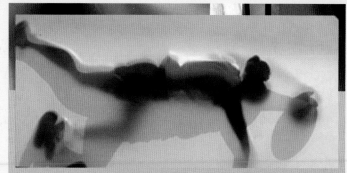

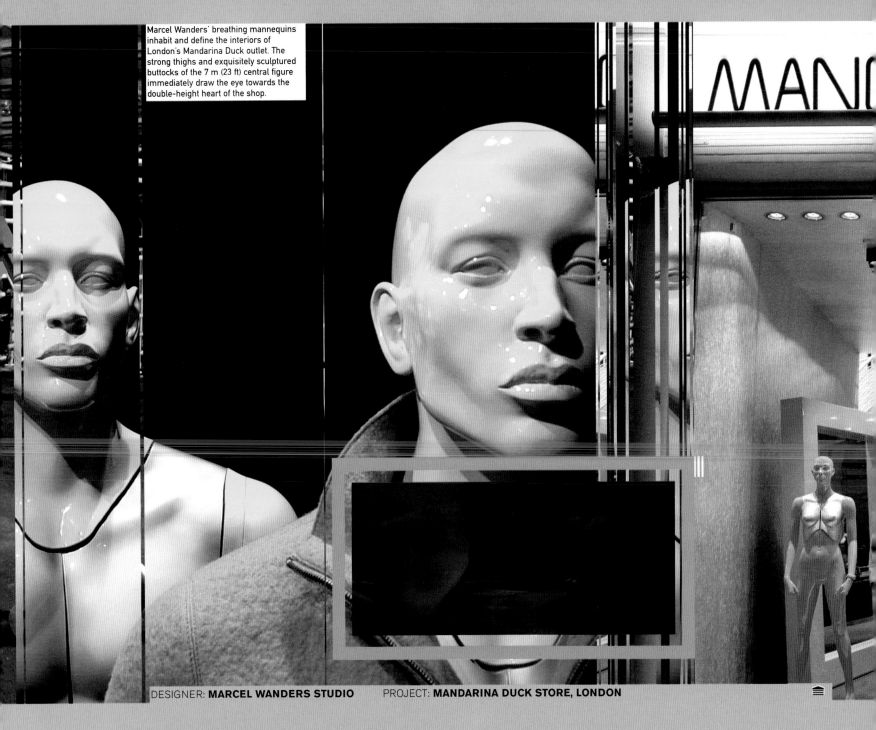

Marcel Wanders' breathing mannequins inhabit and define the interiors of London's Mandarina Duck outlet. The strong thighs and exquisitely sculptured buttocks of the 7 m (23 ft) central figure immediately draw the eye towards the double-height heart of the shop.

DESIGNER: **MARCEL WANDERS STUDIO**   PROJECT: **MANDARINA DUCK STORE, LONDON**

Shops, on the other hand, engage directly with the street, and Marcel Wanders knows his game. This mini-Utopia is meant for all the world to see, to be inspired by and to act upon. The teasing starts from the first glimpse as your taxi swishes you past the store. We are talking theatre of seduction here, in the context of a smart London shopping street.

Wanders' design uses a giant yellow body as both focus and organizer. A figure 7 m (23 ft) high stands within a conventional corner site, so that from the street you get a very good view of his thighs, and you wonder where these oversized muscular limbs could lead. He is no normal giant. Nor is he just any yellow, but Mandarina Duck's identity hue of it.

To keep this fibre-glass giant happy, lots of other, more normally sized male and female mannequins inhabit the two main levels of the shop. Totally naked, this Gulliver in Lilliput dominates the space, while the others wear the clothes or carry the bags, forming a society of yellow people in orbit around him. Their yellowness maintains them in the realm of décor, and offsets the neutral

ARINA DUCK

colours of most of the merchandise. To make them at least part human, and that bit closer to the customers, they breathe. While you graze over the goods in the store, they have an uncanny presence as their metallic chests heave.

Tough and naked, large and small, together these figures define selling space and are the architecture of the interior. Their ploy is to spar with the customer and, with this narrative structure of aliens and giants, to stand in for us. This may sound like quite a jump, but it implies that we, like the mannequins, are helping to

create the environment. Indeed, any conventional interior of walls, floor and lighting more or less disappears into the background. The project drawings serve to reinforce this interpretation. Glancing up to the upper floor, you realize that Gulliver is turning his torso and looking over his left shoulder. His right hand rests on a piece of furniture, and to see this properly you must go upstairs and face him. From the stair, you approach from behind his gaze. Of course, he is looking into the room, as if hinting that we should go and pick over the goods in it.

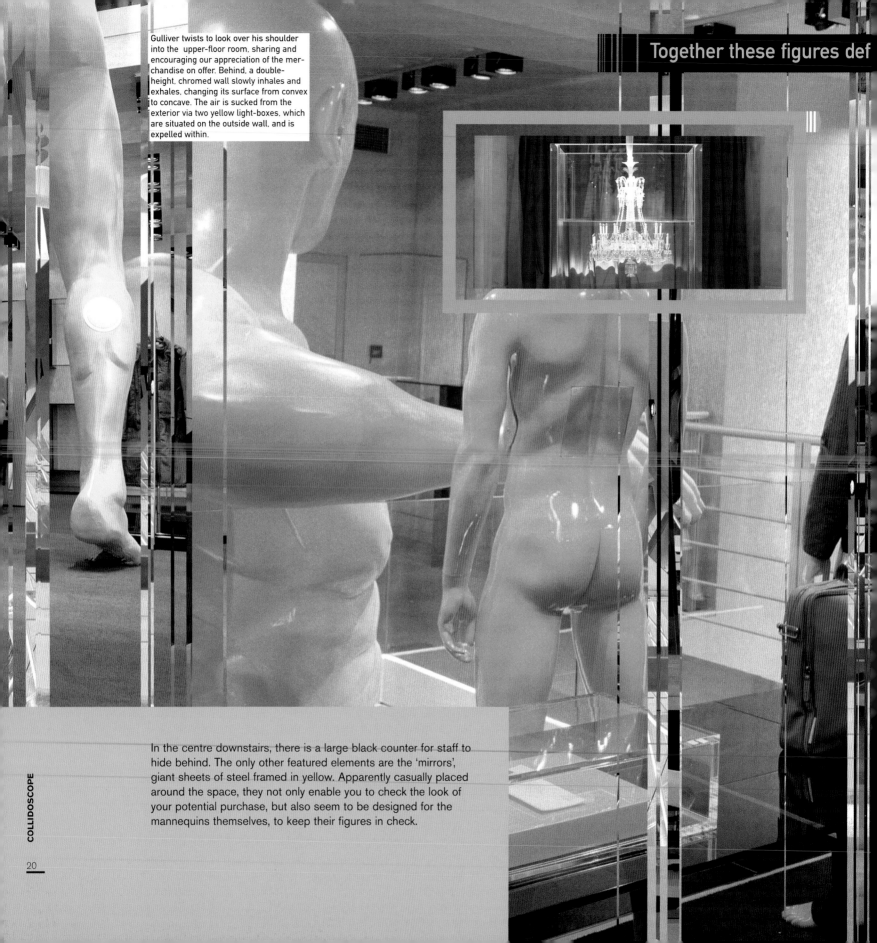

Gulliver twists to look over his shoulder into the upper-floor room, sharing and encouraging our appreciation of the merchandise on offer. Behind, a double-height, chromed wall slowly inhales and exhales, changing its surface from convex to concave. The air is sucked from the exterior via two yellow light-boxes, which are situated on the outside wall, and is expelled within.

In the centre downstairs, there is a large black counter for staff to hide behind. The only other featured elements are the 'mirrors', giant sheets of steel framed in yellow. Apparently casually placed around the space, they not only enable you to check the look of your potential purchase, but also seem to be designed for the mannequins themselves, to keep their figures in check.

Set beneath tempered glass rings, circular neon and halogen lighting is embedded within the two-tone epoxy floors below each dummy. The centrepiece of the store is a floor-to-ceiling sculptural form. This was laser-cut directly from CAD drawings and constructed off-site from lacquer-coated plywood over a rib and gusset substructure.

ARCHITECT: **ASYMPTOTE**   PROJECT: **CARLOS MIELE FLAGSHIP STORE, NEW YORK**

WOMBS

Your mother's womb is the place of your home until birth. It is your first interior, so no wonder you carry its imprint with you. If you are a man, you are an eternal child and never regain that space except in dreams or sexual play. And if you are a woman, it figures as a primordial architecture within your body, a place of intimacy and comfort to be protected at all costs. If a space has been designed to be more like a womb than a room, there are implications for all that is in it, and for those who use it. How should you think of the floors, walls and door?

The Carlos Miele Flagship Store works without emphasis on colour or detail; it is more of a condition, a soft inner chamber that can give birth to the clothes without any contaminating cultural precedent. This may be a common enough intention in the design of clothing stores, but unlike the majority of white boxes that cautious companies have commissioned from designers they do not really trust, Miele and Hani Rashid have gone for a womb-like approach that really does give birth to the clothes.

In Manhattan most of the smartest new fashion shops, such as

Comme des Garçons and Stella McCartney, are in the Meat-packing District on the Lower West Side, and this one has joined the trend. For all of these shops and the many galleries alongside them, the harsh urban setting of the area actually adds to the attraction. Either side of the display windows that look onto the street, utilitarian façades and crumbling pavements contribute to the visitors' sense of discovery.

Inside, the store is a clean yet intimate coalescence of white enclosure, and floors, walls and ceilings seem to melt into one another. But the view from the street is well handled, too. From there you see a featured garment hanging in mid-air. It is surrounded by an ellipsoid frame, which effectively pushes the garment forward towards the viewer and at the same time opens a long view into the core of the shop.

While the clothes combine Grecian draping with jungle prints of Amazonian simplicity, in the shop they hang as if in free space surrounded by loose frames of white. Rashid's design functions as an abstract yet sensuous backdrop to the womenswear by the

The dismembered torsos of the mannequins are lit from above and below. White
against a neutral palette of grey-greens.
their brightly coloured jungle-print dresses appear to float across the ethereal.
sculpted spaces.

Brazilian designer. Each mannequin is headless and on a wire,
and each is lit from above and below, which helps to emphasize
the sculptural quality of the clothes.

With its hollowed forms, the waving wall works as something of a
divider, a seat and a display surface. It is the single most voluptuous element in the whole design, conferring a feminine fluidity
on the whole space. As Rashid explains, this element took most
effort to make. Designed in 3-D digital format, the data from this
was used to make it up in sections that were assembled *in situ*.

All around, the effect of the design makes the clothes float in a liquid, no-hands manner – whether on rail or mannequin, suspended
in a pure white and limpid grey space with no separation between
GRP (glass-reinforced plastic) walls, epoxy floor and stretched
PVC ceiling. Even though it is a public area, shopping here should
be a private experience, with the volumes in the womb-like space
providing constant support. Sensuously formed surfaces flow one
into another, shaping themselves into framing spots for the clothes,
which, once you have chosen, anticipate your rebirth as a star.

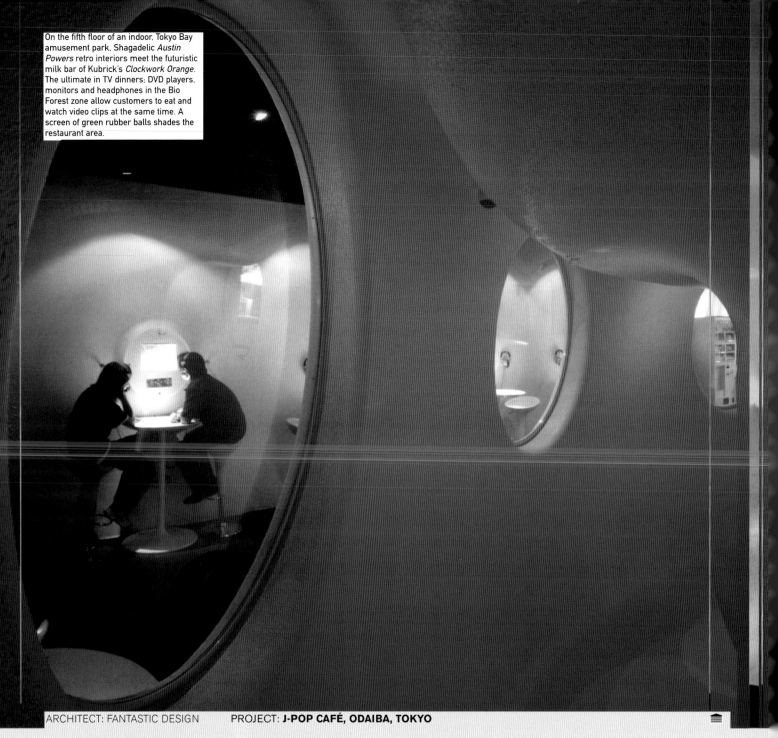

On the fifth floor of an indoor, Tokyo Bay amusement park, Shagadelic *Austin Powers* retro interiors meet the futuristic milk bar of Kubrick's *Clockwork Orange*. The ultimate in TV dinners; DVD players, monitors and headphones in the Bio Forest zone allow customers to eat and watch video clips at the same time. A screen of green rubber balls shades the restaurant area.

ARCHITECT: FANTASTIC DESIGN   PROJECT: **J-POP CAFÉ, ODAIBA, TOKYO**

There is no real centre of Tokyo; even so, this place is far-flung, and that is part of its attraction. As an intrepid trend monkey, you can reach the J-Pop Café by taxi or on the metro. On arrival, you are no longer in the hinterland, but find yourself separated in time and space from the claustrophobia that characterizes so many more normal venues.

Follow those in the know to the fifth floor of Sega's Joy Polis, a mega indoor amusement park that's part of the Odaiba Decks Tokyo Bay entertainment complex near Tange's Fuji Television

building. Here you will eventually find the J-Pop Café. You'd be forgiven for believing yourself to be on the edge of the future, but experiencing something of a déjà vu. This is a place in which to live the 1960s pop culture first-hand, with a mood defined by *Clockwork Orange* or *Stop the Shop*, or by what the designer calls anti-modernist design.

The café is a curvaceous biomorphic series of spaces designed for visitors to watch the latest pop videos and eye up other pop aficionados. On entering, you are greeted by a green screen

made from suspended rubber balls; past this, fast food is on the table for you in seconds, accompanied by the video of your choice. Within its black opencast ceiling and shiny floors, built-in tables and chairs (designed by Karim Rashid) set up individual viewing and eating stations. Complete with adjacent head-phones, monitors housed in circular protrusions from the walls transfer your focus away from the room, into your chosen video. However, the *pièce de résistance* turns out to be the main restaurant, a direct, womb-like space that opens its views onto

Tokyo Bay. Here floors, walls and ceiling, together with the tables and chairs, seem to melt into one another; in fact, they are all made from the same 1960s material – plastic. The thrust of the space is towards the windows, and this sensation is helped by the fact that the floor tips very slightly down towards them. A row of seats follows the curve of the windows but, of course, offsets the panoramic bay view with a host of other video monitors. Despite the café's otherworldly sense of separation, there are clues to the urban density of which this micro-world is a part.

The organic shaped walls contain computer-controlled LEDs, which constantly
change the lighting from red to purple to
green along the passage leading to the
Bio Cave restaurant. An almost entirely
glazed wall gives panoramic views of
Tokyo Bay and vies for dominance with
the long, curving Decola counter.

Great diagonal bracing elements cutting across the windows are
evidence of Tokyo's anti-seismic structures. Even these columns
are incorporated into the jelly bean gloop. They provide a powerful reminder of the continuing conflict between one of the most
intensely packed metropolitan environments in the world and the
natural danger from earthquakes – of which there may be up to
five on the average day.

The gable form of the neon outline emphasizes Giovannoni's concept for the Alessi exhibition during the Milan Furniture Fair 2002. Five houses were constructed, each to demonstrate how the same range of bathroom furniture can be used to differing effect if the language of its setting alters.

DESIGNER: **STEFANO GIOVANNONI**   PROJECT: **BATHROOM EXHIBITION FOR ALESSI, MILAN FURNITURE FAIR 2002**   ≡

Though he trained as an architect, Stefano Giovannoni's real success has come with his work for Alessi. He and his colleague Guido Venturini were responsible for the first Alessi designs in plastic, such as the cockerel-shaped stove lighter and the squirrel nutcracker. His plates with paper-chain cut-outs of children have also been real winners, with the design being translated into over fifty products.

Inevitably Alessi's success at commanding a design gift market meant that more products for the home would be planned, and these would not necessarily be made from the material most readily identified with the company – stainless steel.

A new range of bathroom fittings was to be designed by Giovannoni. It would encompass as complete a range as those of any rival in the field, including bath, shower, WC, bidet, washbasin and extras, such as towel rail and toilet-roll holder.

Perhaps Alberto Alessi had been particularly inspired by the designer's earlier toilet brush, the Merdalino, a bright plastic plant that had to be uprooted from its pot to reveal the brush. This

product is undoubtedly one of Giovannoni's most successful, to the extent that when the new bathroom range was launched in 2001, he erected an oversized one on the corner of the roof of his building. Here the bathroom collection was displayed in a series of custom-made spaces on the ground floor.

I remember coming around the corner and thinking, God, is that his building? It was certainly an impressive one for a design studio, only conceivable in the lucrative design environment of Milan. An enormous ex-power station in futurist style, this building

proved ideal for Giovannoni, enabling him to bring the various strands of his work together under one roof.

For the launch, however, it was billed as the Alessi venue, and provided the focus for a stream of visitors, attending as much to see the building as to admire the new products. In the huge ground-floor space, Giovannoni had built five 'houses', each of a different colour and containing a bathroom installation. Each house served to express one style within a lexicon of what the bathroom could be. These tent-like rooms, with strong colours

The different houses are individually coloured and are characterized by varying materials, such as wood and mosaic. Bright colours and emphatic polychromatic lighting offset the purity and simplicity of the ceramic sanitary ware.

and edges, used the foreground for a different material, such as mosaic, wood and enamel. All were emphasized by coloured light that seeped from gaps between the panels.

The objects themselves have the clean simplicity of Giovannoni's other pieces for Alessi, but not their smiling faces or cartoon character. They are quietly rotund, and would perhaps be at home in the Mini Mouse interior, but they eschew iconic messaging. As any architect turned product designer will suggest, these objects are in themselves enough to define the space around

them as architecture. They can more or less dictate the quality of the interior. Yet the little, tent-like houses are from the Giovannoni book of cartoon architecture. Many other designers would feel at home in them, including the London-based FAT.

The great outdoors is brought inside Tate Modern's home for educational activities. Four pieces of furniture, each with the form of a building or a piece of landscape, stand against a silhouetted skyline painted in pink on the walls.

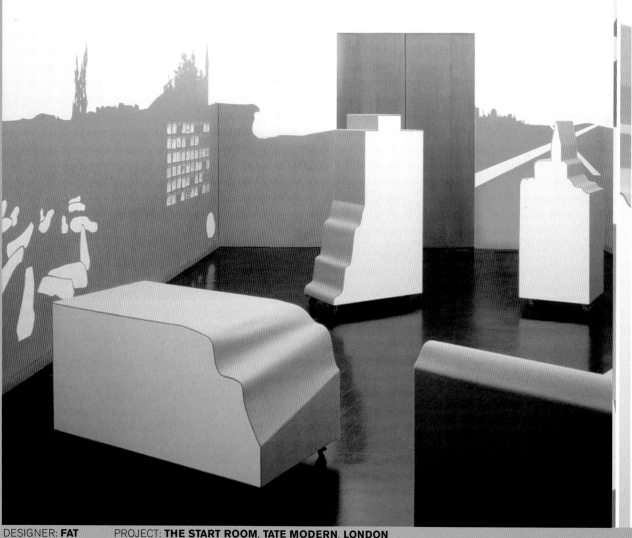

DESIGNER: **FAT**   PROJECT: **THE START ROOM, TATE MODERN, LONDON**

PLAYPENS

For a child, the enclosed pen is a micro-territory of freedom, but as adults we don't play easily. Play is held to be wasting time, a distracting indulgence, but it can be liberating, too, as advertising agencies who depend on creativity have discovered. In our leisure-orientated society, many spaces are dedicated to adult gratification, but they are more powerful when found in unexpected places. At times you need a space apart, a place where things are cartoon-like and abstracted.

This Fashion Architecture Taste (FAT) design plays on being a parallel to the world of art it sits in, but at the same time completely outside its cultural terms of reference. No one thinks of Tate Modern first as a playground, but the playpen is an effective metaphor if you wish to learn more. Come here, as many children on the Art Trail do, and you are free to regress in age and learn by accident. This room is both the start and finish of Tate Modern's learning experience – a place to gain spiritual refreshment and to contemplate the contents of the rest of the building.

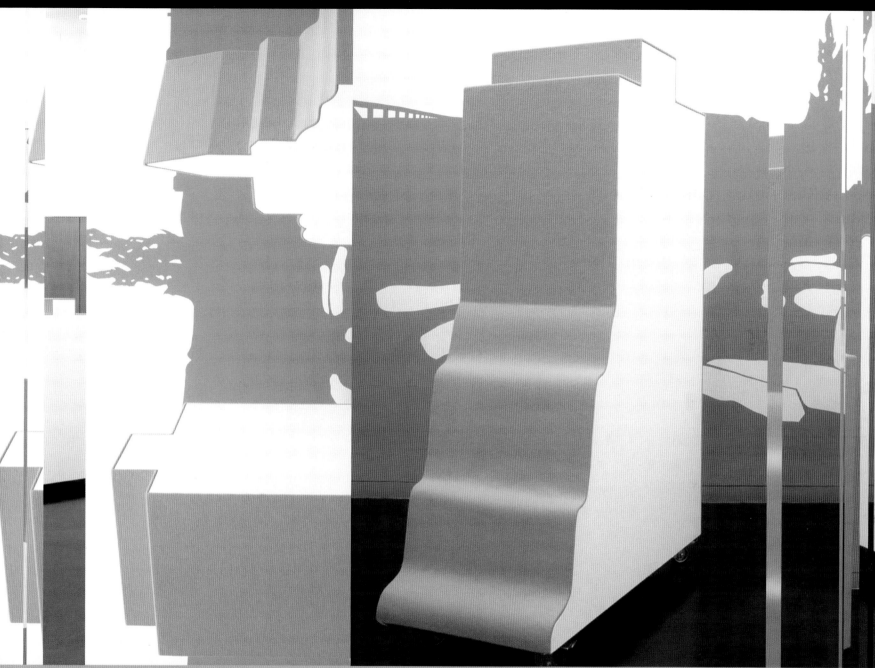

The design, which could not be simpler, consists of a wall painting and four pieces of furniture. The wall forms a horizon around the room, so that when you are in it you want to solve the puzzle – the connection between the four objects: a church on a hill, a slab block and mountain, a hill and a ravine. Each plays with its status as both cut-out and furniture covered in green baize and with its connections to the same outlines on the walls.

FAT's work is consistently bound up in illusions of representation and interpretation. With its games of scale and insistence on architectural cliché, their house in Garner Street, for example, pitches toy-like images of the typical house against the equally typical office block. In landscape design, they are inclined to reproduce elements typically found within it, and play these off some wildcat elements. In this room at Tate Modern they have mixed the two ideas, making large objects that represent much larger features characteristic of the British landscape.

When it comes to toys, cut-outs are a familiar translation of reality into a form that a child can dominate and manipulate. So, though

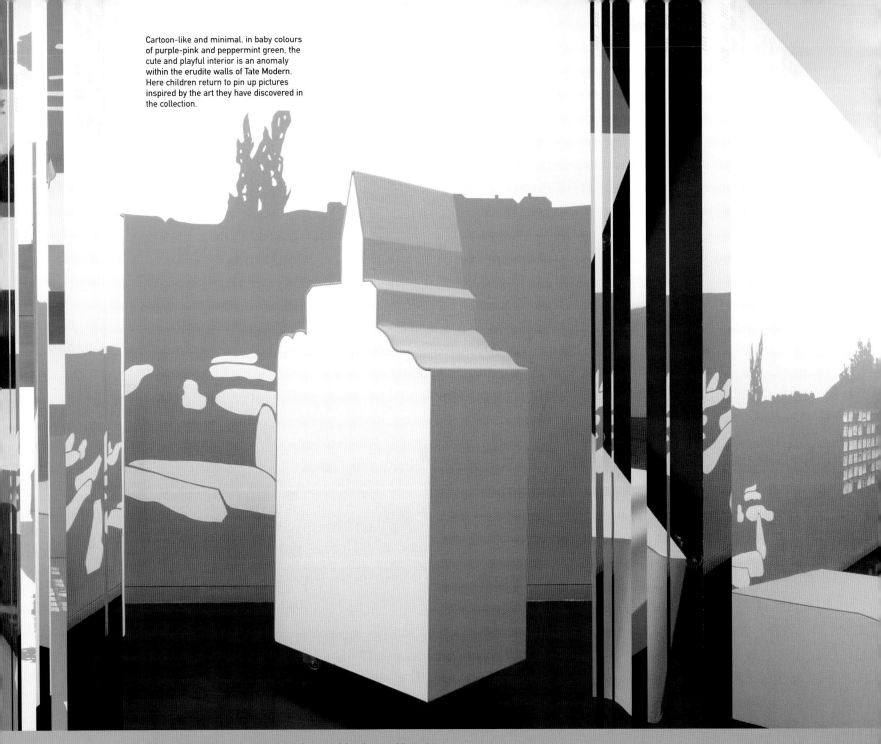

Cartoon-like and minimal, in baby colours of purple-pink and peppermint green, the cute and playful interior is an anomaly within the erudite walls of Tate Modern. Here children return to pin up pictures inspired by the art they have discovered in the collection.

these objects are functioning pieces of furniture with real presence in the room, their cut-out-ness ensures that they can be shuffled in the space. The disconnection of these physical objects from their parallel images on the wall sets an intriguing sculptural discourse in motion.

The complexity of this apparently simple ploy is enhanced by the reference to some of the works of art in Tate Modern's collection. When children return to this space from the gallery, they use the walls to pin up their own drawings of what they have seen.

The boardroom at Winchester Wharf was created as part of a stepping of spaces above and below street level The original windows and openings offer panoramic views over the Thames. Below is a lower-level reception area. This newly created space mixes roughly hewn timber with the delicacy of glass and metal.

DESIGNER: **SOFTROOM**   PROJECT: **FISHERKING DEVELOPMENTS HEADQUARTERS**, **WINCHESTER WHARF**, **LONDON**

Despite retaining their original names, most warehouses along the Thames have either been rebuilt or deprived of their original identity. It is surprising, then, that architects Softroom have succeeded in combining their cyber style with the heavy oak and brick of Winchester Wharf, just opposite the City.

Like many of the best designs, the project was achieved within constraints to the benefit of the whole. In particular, the height restriction of 3.5 m (12 ft), combined with the fact that they could not alter the existing window on the river façade, led Softroom to develop an ingenious solution of interconnecting levels. Fisherking Developments, the client, wanted to eke out as large a workspace as possible from this cramped but elongated volume. So Softroom excavated the space adjacent to the river, allowing a stepping of spaces encompassing the work area below ground, the reception at street level and the boardroom overlooking the river itself.

You enter the space off Clink Street, one of those especially atmospheric alleys in which the majority of the warehouses are

still intact. From here you enter the reception, which is on the intermediary level and so maintains direct contact with the activity going on above and below, adjacent to the river. Wherever you are within the space, you cannot avoid being aware of who else is in it. The aim here was to make everyone working in the building feel connected.

As though it were a tree house, the design exploits the hermetic nature of the inside of this building. Through games of scale and material, it reworks the original volume and its views towards the

Thames. From the dark HMS *Victory* character of the envelope, the old warehouse doors open onto the river. Virtually devoid of river traffic, the view of the Thames has a wonderfully calming effect. Its subtly shifting greys and reflected light serve to animate the spaces that look out. In turn, Softroom have used this as an anchor for the rest of the design, establishing an abstract geometry of slots and solids that pop up throughout the space. Downstairs, for example, a blue dividing wall has a slot cut into it that inverts this river view.

The main office areas retain the exposed brickwork of the original warehouse. A large structural timber spine runs through the centre of the building and extends into the boardroom. The two areas are separated by a glass wall.

Surfaces are clean and minimal but, alongside the beams and cross-bracing of the original building, they define a set of levels that establish a floating, conceptual character in the whole design. Lights exploit the dramatic potential of the beams and columns, providing a new system of beams made purely of light. Some raw materials, such as the concrete surfaces, contrast with the painted planes and the charcoal steel service stack. The finely finished timber floors appear to be devoid of support, offering a subliminal connection to the river outside.

The main bedroom of FAT's Garner Street house is situated above the kitchen/living space (right). It is set back from the front and back elevations, forming a stairwell and lightwell respectively. To the rear is a large fireplace, surmounted by a balustrade with heart-shaped motifs.

ARCHITECT: **FAT**   PROJECT: **2A GARNER STREET**, **LONDON**

The house at Garner Street in East London developed from a competition to design a billboard house – a structure that would incorporate advertising that, in turn, would help to pay for its construction. The façade has three rows of under-scaled windows towards the top, and these sit within a billboard in the shape of a typical house. This combination is an attempt to communicate house and office building at the same time. A second façade, perpendicular to the street, has another equally typical cut-out form. When you see the two together, it is difficult to read the scale of the building. You cannot see exactly where the floors occur, nor can you connect the two façades to one another. Although they appear to be built of lapped timber, in reality these boards are made from cement fibre. These structural games set the scene for the three-dimensional ones that take place inside the Garner Street house. Deceptive in both forms and materials, the house continually challenges the users, in this case the designer himself and his family, to be stimulated by incongruous relationships.

The house is entered through the garden into the kitchen, which is also the main living space. Its exterior is decked and surrounded by a wooden or a brick wall. The pastel colours and flatness of the paint finishes give the space an abstract quality – a stage set of barely comprehensible scale.

You enter the house through the garden. On the ground level, garden, kitchen and living room work as one set of interconnected spaces. Set back from the outside walls, and above the kitchen, one of the bedrooms appears to hover. From the street, you can see directly onto the stair that links the two levels, and see the box that encloses this bedroom. The bathroom is the heart of the house.

There is something of Sir John Soane about the result. On the one hand, the space is a manifesto for FAT, proclaiming the need for architecture to work a level of discovery and absurdity into an everyday vocabulary. On the other, it exploits an art paradigm, through traces of Matta Clark, the New York artist who sliced his way through buildings. Though functional in layout and economic in terms of the use of space, the house succeeds in combining simplicity and surprise. Though at times coming dangerously close to the vocabulary of post-modernism, ultimately the house is very much of our time.

In Softroom's menswear department at Selfridges, suspended structures create a greater intimacy by lowering the perceived ceiling height. Used for brand advertising and display, they are made from a series of powder-coated mild steel angles, welded to form frames. These are infilled by coloured perspex panels and hung from existing soffits on stainless-steel cables.

the hovering structures ligh

DESIGNER: **SOFTROOM**   PROJECT: **MENSWEAR DEPARTMENT, SELFRIDGES, MANCHESTER**

TABLES

Whether inside or out, we are so familiar with the ground because we live in relation to it all the time. In bed, the 'ground' is soft; in crossing the city you walk on stone or Tarmac, grass or carpet. But what if the ground surface were to split and occupy a different level? A swimming pool doubles the ground; the water's surface is a paradigm for it. A space can combine 'real' ground with another lifted above – as if a table has grown to room size in height and breadth.

Most department stores play on choice and the value of the selection, but one vast room full of clothes can be disorienting. Selfridges wanted to keep such openness, but at the same time make their new menswear department attractive to upmarket brands and shoppers alike. The vast scale of the store needed to contrast with a more boutique-like sense of intimacy, while maintaining a sense of connection to the store as a whole.
Architects Softroom have used the height of the space to generate the design. Chief designer Oliver Solway explains that the

COLLIDOSCOPE

46

idea was to double the space by building a second ground suspended above the floor. Rather than enshrine the clothes themselves with subdivisions, he has devised a way of giving this open space definition with a series of empty rooms that hover above it. These contain lights and translucent layers of colour, to one side red and the other yellow, and offer opportunities for branding and display.

With a graphic and lifestyle language of contemporary men's fashion, this solution not only creates an otherworldly, Piranesian atmosphere of vastness and theatricality, but also provides a rational way of reading the space and merchandise. The hanging rails and display units have an overt bent-metal simplicity that imparts a warehouse mood and means that the department can easily be reconfigured to suit new merchandising stories.

Unlike Softroom's more curvaceous work, the structures here work with rectilinear forms. However, the result is surprisingly similar. Their net effect is to cross-ply the space with a Matrix-like sense of movement and anti-gravity. These hovering structures

The display fittings are clipped into the ceiling and onto the floor, and can be moved as desired. This flexibility allows the individual areas to change accordingly to reflect the quality, layout and density of products displayed.

lighten the floor by uncluttering it, and lighten themselves by being virtual rooms. Though shoppers will hardly be meditating on the interior – they will be much more interested in the clothes themselves – the panels, beams and openings appear to lift the lid on the vast number of garments hanging on the rails.
This project has a connection to the work of artists who use geometry and transparency, such as Liam Gillick or Jorge Pardo. Both of them pile up orthogonal geometries to the point of stimulating a sense of irrational complexity that embraces modernism,

yet goes beyond it. This may be why in this project Softroom have used colours that are both modernist and artificial. The ceiling is black and washed with concealed blue light. This offsets the suspended cabins, with their white structure, and the fluorescent panels, which stand out from the darkness above.

Organic, fluid and amorphous shapes are often used by Karim Rashid, who admires their sensuality and warmth. In Morimoto restaurant, the Japanese model of semi-private dining has been adapted by using booths with leather benches in the centre of the space, and lining the walls with individual seating. The relief is made from a semi-gloss stucco on top of metal lathe.

DESIGNER: **KARIM RASHID**   PROJECT: **MORIMOTO, PHILADELPHIA**

In this age of poly-culture, Japanese restaurants no longer need to make you feel as though you are in Japan for the evening. All that minimal stuff went with the first round of discovery, but now some clients want to distinguish themselves in other ways, and Morimoto braves it by working with the contrast between excessive order and its breakdown.

Rashid worked his design as a response to an awkward space, some 65 m (213 ft) long, 7 m (23 ft) high and 8 m (26 ft) wide. He built a grid of booths across the floor and contrasted them with a much more sensuous treatment of the walls, which have become digital clouds.

Rashid always has a playful sensibility, but here we see him working this through in an uncharacteristically logical way, testing the relationship between the essentially hard nature of the built environment and the capricious nature of people. Put diners in pens, and they will definitely be up for escaping from them. They love the tantalizing play between hard and soft. The design exploits the fact that the height of your waist more or less equals the

A view of the dining area from the mezzanine at Morimoto. The Cartesian grid of tables and booths is contained by, and contrasts with, the biomorphic relief on either side of the dining area. LEDS embedded in the frosted Italian glass partitions between tables change colour every quarter of an hour.

height of the chair back. Rashid has used this break between the upper and lower torso to differentiate the organized space of dining from the dizzier space in the upper half of the room.

This grid of booths is leather-lined and topped by sheets of internally lit glass. Each seating surface cantilevers from a little wall, internally lit with coloured light. The colours change as the evening progresses, going through six distinct colours every 90 minutes. By adding many of these walls together, Rashid has constructed a luminous battery of pens. Sitting in any one of them enables you to feel both protected and private from the neck down, yet invigorated by the huge artificial sky from the neck up. Clouds billow across the walls, and light sprays out from behind them.

Working across this division between the upper and lower strata creates a tension between mind and body. The fact that the tables are packed into a grid gives you the sense that the space has been split – and that so have you, the visitor. It is as though the whole is divided by a giant table surface. It is a pity that these pictures cannot express the changes of atmosphere and the movement of the people in the spaces. Diners are the missing parts of this architecture. When the restaurant is full, you peer across a constantly shifting sea of animated heads. Seeing the restaurant without them is rather like looking at an empty plate.

The Dutch Pavilion is a private lounge situated in a public environment. Vetted at the door, select groups are invited inside, where they can take their shoes off and relax. Allowed to customize their environment, visitors can control the light, seating, audio surround and climate. They can also select what they view on 8 television sets, each offering 8 channels.

DESIGNERS: **NL ARCHITECTS AND BERND DRUFFEL**   PROJECT: **PRIVATE CITY/PUBLIC HOME**, VENICE BIENNALE 2000

NL architects took over the Dutch Pavilion at the 2000 Venice Biennale of Architecture with a project that enabled people to 'live in public'. Their concept gave expression to the architects' belief that 'new developments in technology and society have blurred the clear distinction between public and private'. It presented two distinct spaces, the NL lounge and the World Wide Web, interactively linked to one another. The architects wanted to represent the world in terms of service, facility, connection and communication, while creating an installation that would be both comfortable and alienating at the same time.

The design of Private City/Public Home cleverly combines the polemical qualities of an art installation with those of an everyday facility. It relies for its ambience on a level of straightforward user friendliness – and you could see that the people who used it felt very much at home. However, usage would gradually release a disquieting set of questions, including the need for the home to be private. What was it that you could not do here?

A security camera surveys everyone who enters the pavilion. (In 2000, for the first time, individual national pavilions were responsible for their own security.) This is an indication of the move

towards privatization. Public space is more private than ever. The design exploits the unifying notion of the ground, with adjustable beds let into it. Visitors were invited to remove their shoes on entry, preparing them for the relaxation on offer. Large images are projected on the wall, and once inside people are free to enjoy the informal atmosphere of the lounge. You can adapt the so-called Auping beds into lounge chairs, dim or turn up the lights, select any TV programme or tune in to the Internet. The floor is laced with technology so that it can change form and channel information in individually controlled ways. A Sound

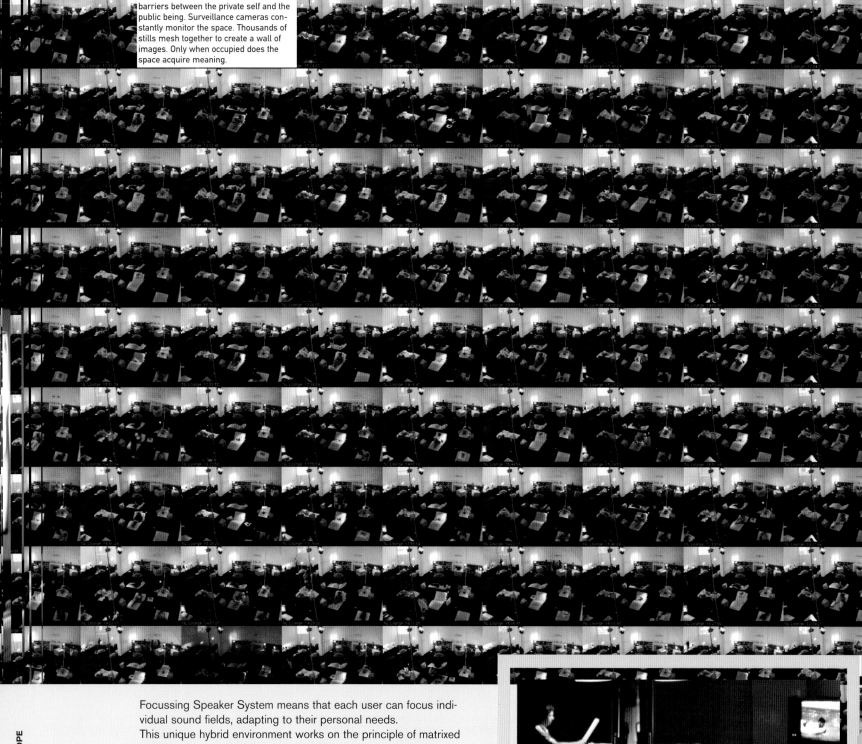

The World Wide Web has broken down barriers between the private self and the public being. Surveillance cameras constantly monitor the space. Thousands of stills mesh together to create a wall of images. Only when occupied does the space acquire meaning.

Focussing Speaker System means that each user can focus individual sound fields, adapting to their personal needs.
This unique hybrid environment works on the principle of matrixed territory within the confines of a specific space. It is not a conventional ground, but a technologically elaborated surface that defines the interior through multiple possibilities. The multiple pictures of the space in use summarize its spirit and the importance of occupation. Why are so many interiors photographed without any sign of people in them?

Abet Laminati's exhibition for the Milan Furniture Fair 2003 invited a number of designers to experiment with digitally created surface patterning. Based on traditional dress-making patterns, El Ultimo Grito's contribution makes the decoration the point of the laminate itself, creating substance from styling. A total of 50 objects can be made from the blueprints printed on the surface.

DESIGNER: **EL ULTIMO GRITO**   PROJECT: **'ALL IN ONE' FOR 'DIGITALPRINT', EXHIBITION, MILAN FURNITURE FAIR 2003**

SHEETS
A sheet on the bed covers the mattress, but because of its flexible nature fits to any shape. If adapted, this flexible surface can move to the ceiling, the walls, over objects – even to the body. The warp and weft of woven fabric enables patterns and representations to be woven into the structure. With wallpaper or paint, surface covering used to be part of the interior, but many new forms of decoration, such as fabric, incorporate repeated colours and design into their surfaces.

El Ultimo Grito have cleverly exploited the booth format of the exhibition, of which this room was a part. They knew that the spaces would be completely artificial, and would set up stage-like scenarios, not so much for living but rather to expound an exercise in communication. The brief for the 'DigitalPrint: A New Generation of Surfaces' exhibition was to design a new printed laminate that exploited the possibilities of an extremely large pattern repeat. Each designer was given a room to try out the result in a 3-D environment. El Ultimo Grito wanted to explore how a

laminate could be both decorative and useful, and to illustrate that pattern could also contain information.

El Ultimo Grito's laminate contains the parts necessary to make up a whole set of furniture pieces. It is based on the idea of traditional dress-making patterns, in which the various shapes that make up garments are printed on top of one another and are selected for cutting by their user. The components for each object are outlined in a distinct colour, so that the outlines for, say, 'chair A' would be in yellow and 'table C' in green. In all,

some 50 designs contributed to the laminate design, each one defined in its own coded colour. Laminate is an acknowledged favourite of many DIY practitioners, and the concept exploits this by suggesting how you could use the laminate to build almost any piece of furniture for the home.

Such an interpretation parallels the idea of selling a complete range of furniture. Using the material to cover the walls adds a further sense of its universality and of the slightly perverted notion that this single substance can define an entire world.

SHEETS

59

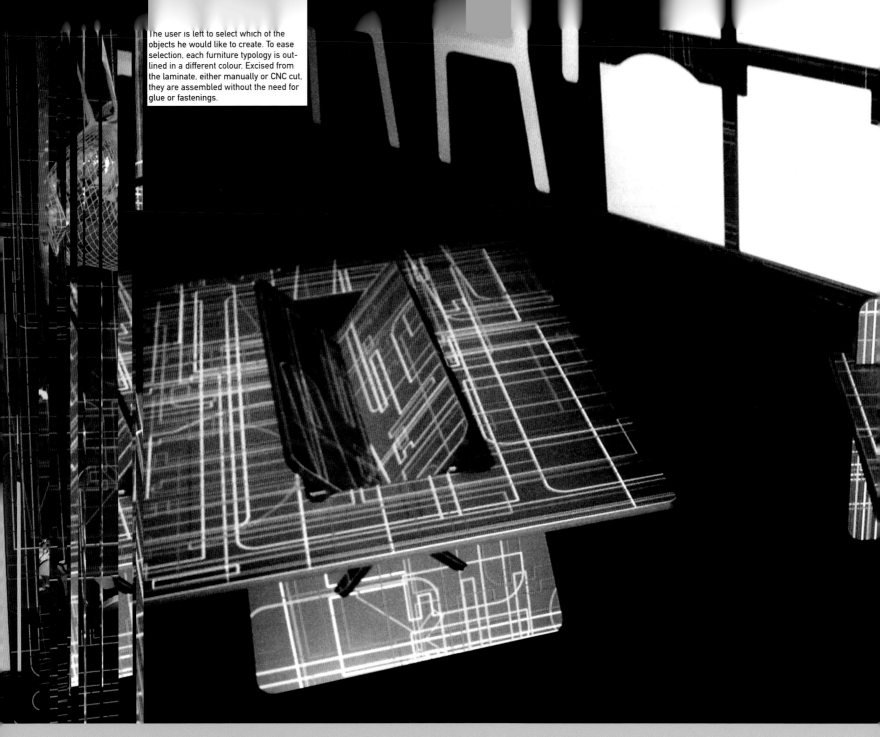

The user is left to select which of the objects he would like to create. To ease selection, each furniture typology is outlined in a different colour. Excised from the laminate, either manually or CNC cut, they are assembled without the need for glue or fastenings.

When you enter the room, the pattern on the walls has so many colours in it that at first it appears brown. On closer inspection, however, you realize that this is merely the effect of so many unrelated multi-coloured lines crossing and interfering with one another (like the warp and weft threads of woven fabric) against their dark background.

The dim lighting in the room adds to a sensation of suspension. This is a familiar experience on the computer screen, when designing with a CAD system. In this dramatic, artificial space, the lines appear to float in a televisual way. This effect is enhanced by the fact that some components have literally been cut from the sheets on the walls, and used to build some of the objects in the room. The space includes a chair, a table and some flower containers, which are attached to the wall.

More like a domestic library than a shop, the bookshop has a homely feel to it. It is furnished with designer pieces, including work by Alvar Aalto, Marcel Breuer and Nick Dine. The spines of the books echo the muted pastel colours of the tiles used on the floor and columns.

DESIGNER: JORGE PARDO   **PROJECT: DIA CENTER FOR THE ARTS, NEW YORK**

Track slightly sideways to Pardo's installation at the DIA Center for the Arts, and you can witness the effect of offbeat colours within a geometric framework causing a sense of contaminated purity. The dramatic coloured tiles kick in even as you cross over the threshold from the street. Cleverly, Pardo has made one installation that crosses two territories, divided only by an L-shaped glass wall with strict aluminium fenestration.

The DIA building houses one major installation by a single artist on each of its five floors, but since Pardo was offered the ground floor, he has also managed to encompass the gallery's other function, namely to accommodate a bookshop. Most artists would have wanted to keep the commercial business of selling books away from their work, but Pardo has done the opposite, and exploited the possibilities of looking across from one to the other. On the smaller side of the wall is the gallery bookshop, and on the other is the gallery.

Pardo's narrative describes the average family home, taken to the point of exploring its dysfunction. Signs of this home populate

both the bookshop and gallery sides, but unlike the user of a real home, you cannot move directly through the glass wall from one to the other. Only the lobby connects them. You are forced to experience the absolute separation of one space from the other, and yet to see them together as a whole. Both spaces share the same surface treatment, and the same sense of light and colour. The installation uses a quarter of an acre [1 hectare] of luminous tiles, custom-made in Mexico. In colours of cerulean blue, red, mustard and avocado, the tiles lock into one another's rectangu-

lar forms. The extent of the tiles is uncompromising – they run across the floor and scale the columns.

Despite this aesthetic continuity, the atmosphere is quite different in each half of the ground floor. The bookshop has the feel of a child's playroom, with the books distributed like toys on a collection of 1950s chairs and sofas, as if in a living room.

Conveniently, the shopper can sit there and read – comfortably if conspicuously. In this state of mind, the effects of the coloured tiles will probably merge with the random colours of the spines of

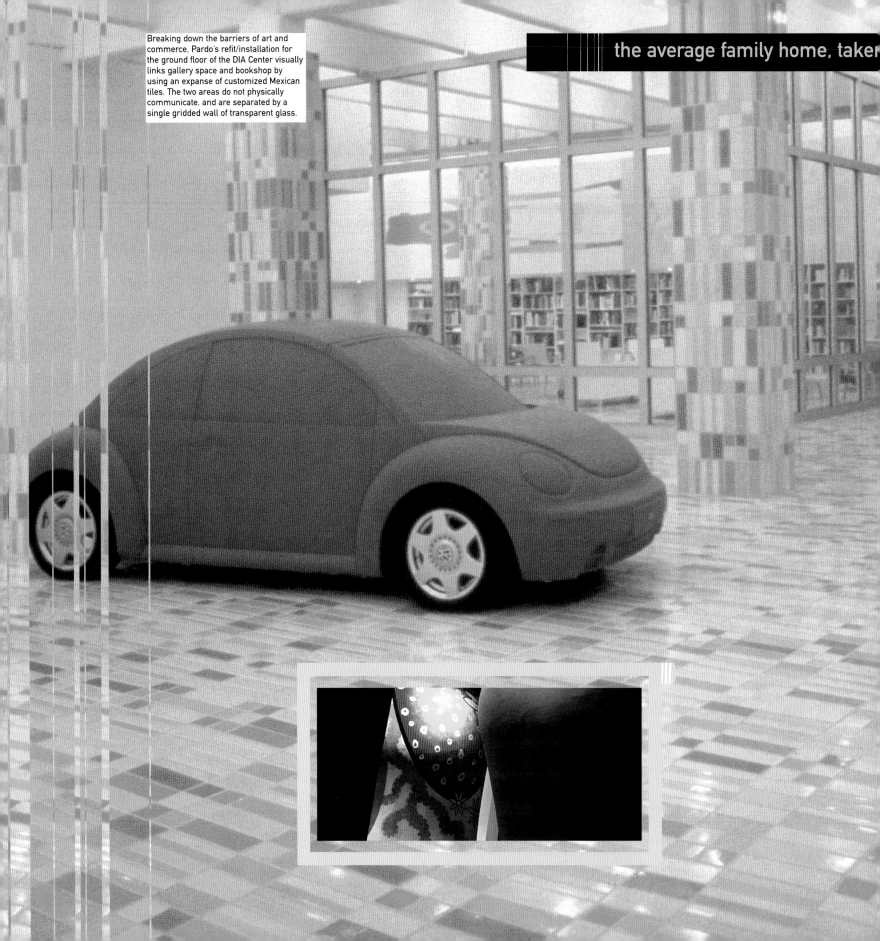

Breaking down the barriers of art and
commerce, Pardo's refit/installation for
the ground floor of the DIA Center visually
links gallery space and bookshop by
using an expanse of customized Mexican
tiles. The two areas do not physically
communicate, and are separated by a
single gridded wall of transparent glass.

the books on the shelves, which define two sides of the room. In contrast to the dignity and contemplation of the bookshop, you are likely to be in more direct contact with the gallery on the other side of the glass. Here there are no comfortable, relaxing chairs. A velvet-covered VW Beetle occupies centre stage, as if outside and in the yard, but its windows are blocked. You are unable to see inside it, and the car, for its part, has exchanged any ability to move for its inanimate sculptural state.

SHEETS

The highly reflective surfaces of marble, glass and Plexiglas serve to create a space-age effect. A whiter than white, or 'optical white', is created by fluorescent tubes concealed in ceiling channels and along the base of the display cabinets, which cast a clear blue light onto the walls and the floors.

ARCHITECTS: **ANDRÉ AND COQUELINE COURRÈGES WITH JEAN BOTTINEAU** PROJECT: **COURRÈGES HQ, PARIS 2000**

Enthusiasts of André Courrèges' clothes will know that when they first emerged in the early 1960s, they expressed the architectural ideas of the time – simple forms inspired by plastics and graphics that ironed out the difference between materials, and reflected the broad inspiration of space travel. Chain-mail dresses made up from dozens of metal discs did not so much contain the woman as translate a proto-cyborg into a strident image of female autonomy. It follows, then, that Courrèges' new showroom should translate some of these ideas into interior terms.

Architecture has always been on the agenda for Courrèges. André is not enamoured of walls – as he says, he spent a lifetime pulling them down – and this principle of openness and connection is more than evident in the new showroom design by Jean Bottineau. It is complemented by the distortion of the walls that do remain, which are offset with plated screens and transparent surfaces. Their luscious and textured pastel surfaces create a floating, almost liquid ambience that spells purity.
Together, this prismatic sequence of interiors houses shop,

In the office spaces, transparency and reflection are enriched by walls of vivid colour. Furniture appears either to float or disappear. Cotton-covered seats rest on Plexiglas bases, tables in clear glass are noticeable only by their cut edge and a mirrored ceiling plays with perception of scale and space.

showroom and offices. The merchandise is an important part of the interior, as are giant images that key the story back to the female form. These huge photographs add emphasis, and link the current collections to the legacy of the fashion house. The effect of these images is to add a staccato of abstraction to the necessary figuration of the clothes themselves. Clothing pieces hang on walls as if sculptures, and these are magnified by giant photographs adorning doors or positioned at the end of corridors. Within this fine Parisian *hôtel de taille*, Courrèges have built a

palace of light, reflection and colour that includes precious materials like marble and glass. Evangelical conviction infuses everything, from the clothes to the environment. Beyond the usual ambitions of design, in fashion, their world must be defined as unquestionable, and here is no exception. The interior would have you believe that the word of Courrèges is the only doctrine. It generates a magical world of sweetness and light, a realm of naive optimism, in which no doubt the staff and customers are all players. Everything and everybody is clad in white or soft pastels.

Lightness and transparency infuse every part of these celestial surroundings. Perspex spheres and circular openings abound. The café area has white leather poofs on Perspex boxes and a backdrop of Andromeda-like creatures in the master's clothes. You could be forgiven for thinking you had one foot on the moon.

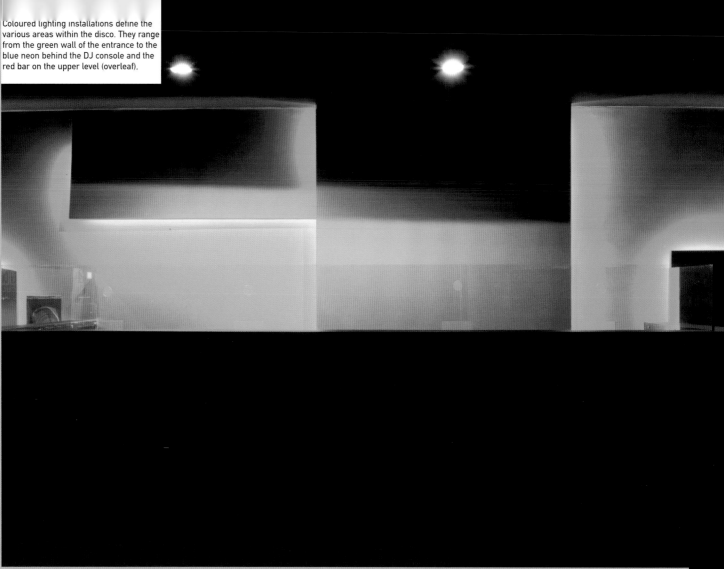

Coloured lighting installations define the various areas within the disco. They range from the green wall of the entrance to the blue neon behind the DJ console and the red bar on the upper level (overleaf).

DESIGNER: **STEFANO GIOVANNONI** PROJECT: **TENDENZA DISCOTHÈQUE, MONTERIGGIONI**

BOXES

The box is the archetypal orthogonal container. You buy things in boxes and keep things in them. You call houses or buildings you may not like after them. But there is an utter simplicity about the box, so just when you least expect it someone wants to make spaces that are more, rather than less, box-like. And then, if you substitute the usual materials for buildings, such as brick and stone, for the fabric, you have the tent, and if you change them for wood, you have the shed.

Monteriggioni, the location for this enormous club, is one of the most intact medieval towns in Italy. From the outside, its complete city walls give the impression of the fortified hilltown that has never succumbed to the enemy. Though the Florentines have long since dominated this landscape, and colluded with locals to exploit it with vineyards and, more recently, factories.

But this club uses another definition of context – the branching 'superstrada' between Florence and Siena. Young Italians are never afraid to drive out of their cities to find the right club. After

all, Rimini has some of the largest clubs in the land. The sea is relatively far from here, and the conurbation of the Arno valley is only minutes away. You can reach Tendenza from Florence in a little over half an hour.

From the outside, Tendenza is little more than a shed, but inside it is a landscape of pure colours. The lightness of these spaces contrasts with the heaviness of the local construction. Each space defines itself through colour, and as such sets up a zone on the mental map created by each of the clubbers.

The purity of the spaces themselves is offset by a further definition of more temporary space – a series of tents, each with its own coloured light and special service offered to the punters inside it. The blue one might be for tarot reading, the red one for a tattoo studio. Tendenza reacts to the principle of the market, though with more emphasis on activities than things. If the old town of Monteriggioni, itself the scene of an annual medieval fair, were to have been under siege, no doubt coloured tents would have stood outside the walls as, over months, the invading army

Traditional tents in the club house various activities, such as body piercing, tattooing and tarot reading. Each is illuminated with a different coloured light, shining like a beacon in the dark, bar area. Adding a touch of cinematic razzmatazz, the stairs (opposite) contain hundreds of little lights within their risers.

sought to intimidate the citizens holed up inside. Today they use tents for quite another purpose – to escape from the pounding music and the constant spectacle of the crowds.

For there is a certain theatricality at work, and the great planes of bright colour are the perfect setting for a TV studio degree. The bars cruise past luminous walls with giant panels that do say bar, but without an actual bottle in sight. You sense that there are no conventional distinctions between walls and floor: the back lit walls reflect well in the polished floors. However, it is the stair-

case that holds the real clue. This wide and steep zigzagging of space has a thousand tiny lights built into its risers. When you see it from across an empty room, it looks rather like a truncated office block, but once the place fills up, the staircase turns into the Folies Bergère.

Flexibility is needed in a space that houses a variety of different exhibitions. Eight movable containers, designed for a series of support functions, slide along tracks. Basic furniture is formed by cutting and folding the container skin inwards. The resultant planes are layered and coated in resin, foam or rubber to create desks, shelves and benches.

DESIGNER: **LOT/EK,**   PROJECT: **THE BOHEN FOUNDATION, NEW YORK**

Not so much a single box as a collection of them, the Bohen Foundation in the infamous and excruciatingly trendy Meatpacking District on the Lower West Side has the endless changing feel of a working warehouse. It has a raw, utilitarian quality that suits contemporary art far better than rooms that have been given the modernist whitewash.

The Foundation occupies a huge space on the ground floor of a warehouse on 13th Street. LOT/EK have a fascination with shipping containers, and not surprisingly have used them here,

together with a clever system of huge sliding panels, to produce a space that they liken to a sound stage. Entering from the street, the first thing you see is a row of containers. You move into the space from the back, like approaching a stage from the wings. Pairs of containers each move back or forth along parallel pairs of track running from the front to the back of the space. There are four towards the back and four at the front, all surprisingly easy to move with one hand. While LOT/EK make little attempt to disguise them, they clearly enjoy cutting and slicing them, and

bending cut sections of wall to make tables and seats. Each of them houses a support space – such as a video room, a reading room and an office.

This leaves the enormous central space to stage the art in the most appropriate way, with the containers working like bookends at either end of the free-forming gallery between them. This can be defined using sets of suspended panels, 5 x 5 m (16 x 16 ft that can slide individually along heavy-duty aluminium ceiling tracks between the containers at each end. They can make just

Reworking the typology of gallery design, LOT/EK have moved away from the idea of an exhibition site being an empty pristine canvas to be filled by artists. Sitting to the back and front of the enormous central space, the containers become part of the installation. Bold graphics add to a painterly effect.

about any spatial configuration an exhibiting artist could want. The whole concept works as a machine for housing art. However it is organized, the gallery has a dynamic atmosphere that complies with the directors' wish for the design to be cheap, exciting and thought-out from first principles. The carcass of the building gets the same brutal treatment as the containers – if the space is still not big enough, part of the floor is covered with removable steel gratings, like trapdoors on a theatre stage. Lift these out and you can instantly add a double height.

When the sliding is fully activated, the space assumes an inherent drama from within. It sets up differences, but it does not comply with the usual hierarchies of diminishing scale, meant to progress from the outside in. Unlike many art spaces, the desire is to show the art in a tough but essentially sympathetic environment. Even though the panels are white on one side, and can define white spaces, the overall colour feel is for the colours of industry. The containers are a stark combination of red and blue, contrasting with the background of brick and raw concrete.

DESIGNER: **SETSUMASA KOBASHI**   PROJECT: **WIN A COW FREE STORE**, TOKYO

When Damien Hirst first exhibited his famous cut-up cow in a gallery space, the art world applauded. However, some critics and newspapers wondered why on earth they should praise a macabre relocation of animal anatomy and, later, of medical exhibits. Yet it resonated, even as far as Japan, as this perniciously accurate reproduction of Hirst's ideas shows.

Hirst himself is well known for his ability to quote the everyday to the extent of encroaching on already charted territory. Witness *Charity*, and his 6 m (20 ft) anatomical figure. However, this installation turns the spotlight on the artist himself, transforming his individual object into a complete environment lined with hygienic cabinets.

Here in Tokyo ideas are up for grabs – often a key point of the city's interiors. And since there is a tradition here of spare presence of the stock, modern wisdom says that you can generate more product placing from the environment than from the products themselves. This concept plays with the juxtaposition of fashion product and dead meat, handled as though in a super-

market or abattoir, which renders the merchandise out of reach, locked in a set of perfectly crafted cabinets. Though the shop has hardly any stock, the point is to match it with some unlikely other objects, and to distance and protect these from the contaminating effects of the customer.

Even the sales desk appears hygienic to the point of clinical, butcher-style cleanliness. Apart from the wheels, its intricate and precise design shows little function from the outside. It exploits its difference from the room as a temporary object, and as such its affinity with the customers. Its itinerant quality renders the room pure, and very nearly without any furniture at all.

Meanwhile the cabinets have a precise industrial geometry that makes the clothes both distant and desirable. This design relies heavily on a specialized catalogue aesthetic – the type of thing that brought stainless-steel prison toilets and lever-arm taps into fashionable circles. Its vocabulary of sensuous alienation brings it close to fetishism, and illustrates the predilection of Japanese design to take its themes to limits hard to match in the West.

Amidst the vast, sleek cabinets, one tiny detail confirms this position. Inside the cabinet on the left, behind the cash desk, there are cartons of drink neatly shelved. These indulge in an ironic exercise of deliberate mis-signification. The drink is packaged in milk cartons, but these are printed with a slice through a carcass – the cartons are, nonetheless, more likely to contain milk than blood.

For their contribution to Swiss Expo 2002, AVL designed an independent free state of wood, scaffolding, tents and tarps on a floating raft constructed from four inflatable emergency bridges manufactured for the Swiss army.

ARCHITECT: **ATELIER VAN LIESHOUT**   PROJECT: **FREE-STATE AVL-VILLE RAFT**, BIEL, SWISS EXPO 2002

SCRAPS

Not all waste is destined for the bin. Scrapped goods can be re-appropriated and used as if new. Rather than the second-hand or recycled, I refer here to the return of the manufactured to a formless state, ready for manufacture again. Scrap is a paradigm for perpetual re-composition and has an aesthetic of its own. When used cleverly to bypass its origin, and connect with other codes of use or meaning, it can undo the discourse of newness while connecting to all things new.

Though not strictly an 'interior', the raft project was intended to be a world in itself. From the outside, you look down upon it as though gazing into the life of a town, or a complex building split apart. It communicates through an interior sensibility. From the sweeping walkway encircling it, the island might as well be the contents of a building rather than a building itself.

Van Lieshout's work explores the fine line between the practical and the absurd, between ugliness and beauty. The environments he creates seem improvised, yet conceived with a forthright

sense of scale that challenges any norms of art or design. Alongside Coop Himmelblau's twisted towers, AVL's Raft or 'Pontoon' seems human and particular – a contemporary caprice based on an alternative to all the effort at social well-being that surrounds it. Looking closer at this gypsy camp, you realize that it is not just self-sufficient, but idealistically disconnected from the world around it.

The island, measuring 24 x 12 m (79 x 39 ft), was, during the six month-long Swiss Expo 2002, an independent free state. For the

duration of the Expo, the raft was accessible to all AVL members and their collaborators, but to no one else. Since it was inaccessible to the public, it did not need to comply with safety rules for public spaces. The structure exploited the fact that with entry limited it could also break all acceptable aesthetics.

According to the Raft's rules, you were not allowed to pollute the water, but you could use the boats, build whatever you wanted, eat, sleep and pursue complete freedom of expression. When leaving, you had to wash up, throw away rubbish, leave the raft

The island is not accessible by the general public and is designed to be viewed from the shore and from the bridge. The DIY aesthetic is the complete antithesis of the clean lines and sterility we associate with Swiss design.

tidy and attractive for the next visitor, and tie everything down on deck. The key was this right to build whatever you wanted. Within the complex were four main structures – the curved Nissen hut the largest and a web of cords and fabric samples the smallest. There was a deliberately chaotic and temporary feel to the whole encampment, emphasized by each of these structures being as much at variance with the others as possible. Inside one of them, the vaulted restaurant, there are no relaxations of the island's absence of aesthetic weakness. Connection to the outside is kept to a minimum, and achieved by prising open the vault to make vertical walls that are suitable for standard windows. Even the furniture had this same insistence on utility. The tables and chairs, for example, were of the type you can source from industrial catalogues.

The BSBbis temporary accommodation is located in a disused furniture warehouse. The small budget, and the fact that the space had to be returned to its pre-conversion state, meant that it was an ideal site for B-architecten's trademark raw aesthetic, which owes more to artistic installations, dirty realism and street culture than it does to interior design.

ARCHITECTS: **B–ARCHITECTEN BVBA**   PROJECT: **BSBBIS, BRUSSELS**

Ever since the theatrical experiments of the Surrealist Antonin Artaud, who declared that the theatre should be nothing more than a hangar, the flounce of traditional sets and of overbearing make-up have been on the wane. Theatre, as opposed to television or film, now finds its strength in raw presentation that bypasses illusion and fakery. Theatre directors want the audience to be as intimately connected as possible to the action, and for theatres to reflect this. The black box is the usual formula, but one group of architects has gone that step further and designed a theatre that is not so much in the round as in the raw.

In Europe's capital of bureaucracy, B-architecten, who named themselves after their Belgian nationality, emphasize their identity as a group rather than a bunch of would-be designer celebrities. They believe that a project rises not from form, but from the constraints that impinge on it. Such is the case with their design for a temporary home for the Brussels Bourse Theatre (BSB).

If there is anything that turns on Crols, Grooten and Engelen, it is a 'hopeless situation', and that may be how things seemed when

confronted by the lack of cash and the empty warehouse that they had been asked to transform. Their approach has been to leave every surface as naked as possible and waste nothing on expensive finishes. The result is a controlled riot of unfinished or stripped-back surfaces, open-meshed screens and the sort of rough edges that you might expect from a building that is only half finished.

If you amble up to the bar, you'll find yourself leaning on a surface made from Stella Artois crates stacked up and finished with

The DIY bar is constructed from stacked Stella Artois crates (below) while the performance area (right) is walled with sandbags. The space, 2,400sq m (25,833 sq ft) in area, is divided equally between two floors, which are connected by a broad slope. It comprises an auditorium, offices and public spaces, which are all treated with the same unorthodox use of prefab industrial materials.

toiletten
toilettes

KO

untreated softwood; and stretched out in a line in front is a collection of standard stools. But there is certainly aesthetic in this apparently DIY combination. The brown and shine of the stools plays off nicely against the red of the crates, the brown of the drinks cabinets behind the bar and the exposed brick beyond. With an overall space of some 2,400 sq m (25,833 sq ft), the theatre has to house auditorium, public areas and offices, and all of these get a similarly direct treatment. The main performance space has walls made from sandbags stacked between lines of

scaffolding poles. The offices, which needed to be cleaner and more defined, are housed in a series of off-the-peg greenhouses. Like many more traditional designers, B-architecten celebrate the combination of colours and materials, but they go for the ones that usually only occur by accident. Together, their theatre's broad mix of conditions coincides in an atmosphere of casual occupancy with an artful disregard for smoke and mirrors.

Kfé
exit
↓

By making visible areas that are normally kept concealed, more light permeates from the bathroom into the kitchen. This flow of light is used to interlock different spaces within the apartment, such as the entry hall (right). Rough-grade plywood of the type normally associated with advertising hoardings has been used throughout the building.

ARCHITECT: BLOCK ARCHITECTURE   **PROJECT: BROOME STREET LOFT CONVERSION, NEW YORK**

When London-based practices take to New York, their awareness of the city is bound to differ from that of local designers. Yet the popularity of lofts in Europe owes its aesthetic to New York. This project by Block is something of a double-take, demonstrating what happens when an English love of irony within the ordinary gets matched to the needs of an American family.

The design borrows from the surrounding environment, yet attempts to accommodate the needs of the individuals who live here. The declared intention of the designers was to enhance the everyday interaction between each of the family members. This was achieved by treating the whole space as though it were itself a city, complete with streets and buildings.

Utility and private spaces are housed behind façades, and the area in front of them works as a continuous shared condition. A through space connects the two ends of the apartment, providing an interconnected series of open rooms. At the heart of this is the kitchen, which is defined with shuttered concrete, rough grained plywood, GRP and back-lit diffused glass. Not one single

space has the usual hermetic character. Although successfully creating privacy when it is needed, walls and furniture slip and slide. Nothing is quite as straightforward as it appears. Translucent storage units in some of the private rooms reveal traces of their contents, while allowing light to cross-filter through from private to public. Occasionally objects transgress their assigned spaces – part of the bath in the 'girls' bedroom' pushes through the wall into the dining room, and the concrete shower wall in the 'boys' bedroom' appears in the study area next to it.

The scale of the loft has been maintained within the main living area (below) and the kitchen (right) which is situated in the centre of the apartment and is the social hub of the interior. Block have used a palette of materials that draws almost entirely from the city outside. Shuttered concrete, rough-grained plywood, GRP and back-lit diffused glass lend the space a utilitarian aesthetic.

Materials that are generic to New York have been throughout the apartment. Products like OSB (oriented strand board) and rough-grade plywood, the type normally found on sidewalk hoardings, have been combined with translucent surfaces to dissolve the difference between the very heavy and the very light. Floor surfaces vary from polished hardwood to MDF. Hinges are unpainted and proudly displayed. Fixings are celebrated, and contrast with painted surfaces and precious woods. Wash-basins are traditionally cubic and the plumbing exposed. Prison bathroom fittings and institutional ones in the kitchen add to the utilitarian hybrid, which links with the harsh masculinity that characterizes so many engineered structures in the city. Light fixtures have been made from standard conduits and junction boxes. There is a deliberate half-finished feel to the whole apartment, but one handled in such a way that the hardness implied by the street is offset by a liberating sense of transparency and leaking light.

Giant, erotically themed images from a series of Jean Nouvel's favourite movies are projected onto the bedroom ceilings and illuminated by uplighters. At night, these scenes are visible from the street through the large windows that define the exterior, making the building one giant filmstrip.

ARCHITECT: **ARCHITECTURES JEAN NOUVEL**   PROJECT: **THE HOTEL, LUCERNE**

MIRRORS

As Narcissus discovered, a mirror can be a tool for performing an act of architecture. But more important than gazing at your own image reflected is the fact that the space is doubled, perfectly and symmetrically, on either side of the surface. The conundrum is that the mirror occupies its own visual axis and we can only occasionally line up to it. Put simply, mirrors elaborate the effects of enclosure. They are counterfeit perforations, and alter your sense of occupation.

Unless you include the love category found in Japan, hotels, by definition, tend to be bourgeois places. The hotel room is meant to fit your values of lifestyle, commodity and comfort. You should feel reassured by that painting on the wall. It should be a little like home, but that bit better. You are also meant to feel as though you are living with servants to attend to your needs. You never know, or want to know, who has been in that bed before you. Everything should be clean and tidy, and for your sake rather than for the management's.

The rooms are elegantly and simply appointed. An exercise in good taste, they act as a foil to the naked cavorting on the ceilings above. The Hotel is not just a place to sleep, but also a stimulating environment with which to engage.

But at The Hotel, this composure might be interrupted by a stocking-clad lust-wanderer. You are never alone here. Every room has a ceiling with some intimate naked figures – your avatars, watching over your stay. Even from the street you can see risqué scenes from some of Nouvel's favourite erotic films projected on the ceilings of all 25 rooms. Passers-by will see these giant images at night, unless occupants decide to close the shutters. Nouvel has chosen these fragments from films by Buñuel, Bertolucci, Almódovar, Lynch, Fassbinder, Fellini,

Greenaway and Oshima. Although deliberately art house in character, their effect is decidedly erotic, and might stand in for tuning in to the erotic channel on the rooms' built-in televisions. The relatively dark and spare design of the rooms encourages environments of role play – all the more so because the images are projected on the ceiling, mirroring yet oblivious of antics below. Sooner or later you take over as the prime performers in your own movie, not even sure in turn that no one is watching you. Nouvel gives careful thought to contrasts of scale and situation.

When you are standing still or walking around, the objects and surfaces you encounter are clean and undecorated. Views from the window are direct and open. No cloth clutters the windows, and the bed linen is simple and straightforward.

One of Nouvel's consistent themes is the removal of boundaries by displacing the internal and external perceptions of a building. Another is the creation of puzzles using spaces and images. These concepts underlie all his buildings, but it is at The Hotel that they have found their most accessible expression.

Down in the bar/restaurant, people seated along the banquette are encouraged to be voyeurs, enjoying tangential views of those up at ground level on the street. Thanks to an elaborate system of mirrors, you can combine intimate chat with your cocktail partner with a periscoped view of the scene above.

Starck's design for Baccarrat's flagship store has given the 240 year-old company a new image. While respecting the interiors of the eighteenth-century mansion, he has added Surrealist and Dadaist touches, references to the building's former owners, who were patrons of these arts from the 1920s until the 1950s. A lit chandelier floats in a giant aquarium (right).

DESIGNER: **PHILIPPE STARCK**   PROJECT: **BACCARAT FLAGSHIP STORE, PARIS**

A veritable feast of glass awaits the visitor to the new Maison Baccarat in the seizième district of Paris. With over 3,000 sq m (32,291 sq ft) of space, it celebrates the grand heritage of this *hôtel particulier*, once the home of the infamous Marie-Laure, Viscountess de Noailles. As a patron of the Surrealists, she financed Luis Buñuel's *L'Âge d'Or* and Jean Cocteau's *Le Sang d'un Poète*. Both of these films were shown in the staggeringly ornate ballroom. Cocteau, whose film *Orphée* exploits the famous image of passing into the Underworld through the surface of a

mirror, would have understood Starck's revelling in the potential of mirror and crystal.

As an apotheosis of any shopping experience, this ensemble of loosely defined retail spaces fully exploits the glamorous narrative of the house. Baccarat designs, always considered the height of luxury and at times of frivolity, are here restored to the ideal scenario in which to view them and, at least in the imagination, to use them. This environment complies with the Surrealist spirit. Oversized, *Alice in Wonderland* furniture dominates the space –

a mirrored throne stands 2.5 m (8 ft) high on the ground floor, while a crystal table, 13.5 m (44 ft) in height, forms the centre-piece of the 'transparent' room. This is laden with classic and recent collections of crystal tableware.

In this suitably grandiose atmosphere, where every theatrical ploy has been applied with relish and skill, members of the public can pore over the lengthy production techniques of the Baccarat company. The diverse exhibits range from their many glass products to magnificent historic chandeliers.

A huge torch-bearing arm adds to the surreal effect. The ground floor contains home, decoration accessories and jewels, displayed in glass cases that contrast with the plain, beige concrete walls (right). A private lounge exhibits historical pieces designed for Tsar Nicholas II and the maharajas of India.

Baccarat has been in business since the time of Louis XV, and Starck makes the most of the decadent inclinations of a court obsessed with luxury. Throughout the house he plays with scale and sugary make-believe, adding individual twists that heighten the sense of the bizarre. In some places he uses raw finishes such as concrete, which support several vast mirrors that sprout human arms bearing torches.

In the first-floor restaurant, the exposed brickwork contrasts dramatically with gigantic baroque gilt frames, satin banquettes

and blown-up, wall-hung cameos in almond pink. Elsewhere, a chandelier glows half-submerged in water; on the stairs hangs another giant one that rotates.

Paris, like London and to some extent New York, thrives on the conversion of buildings. Only some designers, with Starck perhaps the most eminent, know how to breathe new life into an old building by making exaggerated reference to its past. All too often the previous codes, which actually inspired the building in the first place, disappear in the new construction without a trace.

Hani Rashid's design is a reflection on current trading floors as well as provocation for a new, physically augmented environment. The main element is dominated by a back-lit surface of curved and tilted blue glass that creates the feeling of a liquid backdrop.

ARCHITECT: **ASYMPTOTE**   PROJECT: **NEW YORK STOCK EXCHANGE, ADVANCED TRADING FLOOR, NEW YORK**

For some time Hani Rashid had been undertaking research at Columbia University to explore the possibilities of a totally virtual architecture. Would you be able to apply similar criteria of legibility, proportion and function to a virtual environment as you might do to a physical space? Rashid and his fellow researchers thought so, arguing that the common medium was space, and that if a virtual environment was to use this paradigm, there was no reason why the architect shouldn't be the best professional to give it form. For the commission to design a virtual stock exchange, he had the added advantage of being interested in spatial behaviour and film-making. He was the man for the job. When Rashid was contacted by the NYSE (New York Stock Exchange), engineers had been working on the problem for some time. They had heard about his research and wanted him to take on the project, which meant not only designing the virtual environment, but also the place in which it was to be installed. The virtual stock exchange is an advanced trading floor operation centre housed in a custom space designed by Rashid that is an

offshoot from the trading floor of the New York Stock Exchange. Very movie-like in quality, reminiscent of Kubrick's *2001*, it's the big brother of all those urban control centres that monitor traffic. It incorporates a huge number of plasma screens that sweep across a curved wall designed as a continuous workstation. The whole is conceived as an undulating surface with the monitors and controls built into it. Intended by the Exchange to provide a means to model data coming in from many sources, the Advanced Trading Floor (ATF) provides a constantly updating

The curvature of the glass and double-curved work surface, together with the floating plasma monitors that resemble a digital fresco and embedded message boards in the surrounding surfaces, work to create a smooth and seamless space.

a curved blue wall with a gia

interface with the Stock Exchange. It uses complex data management through VRML (Virtual Reality Markup Language), and translates this into a representational system that mimics the real Exchange. However, the ATF visualizes circumstantial data, such as news items and property values, so that it can become part of the trading profile. This enables a higher degree of penetration and prediction of the markets than would otherwise be possible. Rather like a weather-prediction computer system, it provides insight into trends that affect the markets on an ongoing basis.

Although hard to grasp from a series of still images, the ATF is itself a digitally driven interior that literally never stands still. Plasma screens are the key hardware component for these digital spaces; dozens of them hang from lightweight steel structures that curve like the inside of the eyeball towards the viewer. A curved blue wall with a giant oculus in the centre organizes all this data. The virtual stock exchange itself is displayed on just nine of these plasma screens. The rest are used for monitoring data in more conventional ways.

COLLIDOSCOPE

Although occupied by Coates for over 30 years, his apartment is still evolving. He describes the space as an eclectic mix of sensuality, reference and intellect; it is full of objects and furniture either designed by himself, friends and colleagues or collected over the years.

DESIGNER: **NIGEL COATES**   PROJECT: **NIGEL COATES' APARTMENT, LONDON**

DISGUISES

As one of the essential techniques in the art of seduction, an interior thrives on deceit. There is no such thing as truth in architecture – whatever is put forward hides some other angle. London's Victorian façades are neither Roman nor Venetian. Of the many forms of cultural disguise, the most basic is camouflage, as when overscaled graphics are designed to override specific features and so deceive. In interiors, they blur out the form into a naturalistic kind of formlessness.

This sunny apartment has been my home since 1971. All my friends have moved several times, but I have stayed put. The apartment occupies the entire first floor of a corner house in the busy part of South Kensington near the Underground station. Instead of designing it as a precise project, I allowed the place to evolve. Its current manifestation brings together the classical typology of the space with twists and additions that reflect my instinct for sensuality, reference and intellect. This spirit of interference has to work alongside programmatic problems, such as

The entrance is of central importance, acting as a room in its own right and an area from which other spaces unfold. It has recently been painted with a camouflage pattern in the Florentine greys and white that articulate the rest of the flat.

the kitchen, bathroom and bedroom all being tight spaces hidden at the back, the huge extent of windows and the consequent lack of storage.

The entrance is the turning-point of the space, providing both a room in its own right and a lantern from which the other spaces unfold. I asked my painter friend Stewart Helm to give it a camouflage treatment that rides over most of the architectural details, apart from the two original, silver-leafed double doors that open into the sitting room and the dining room. This camouflage reflects the whites and Florentine greys that articulate the whole flat. All of the rooms still have their original mouldings and large French windows, which give the space a feeling of openness and direct contact with the street. The finest original feature is the carved marble fireplace. Thanks also to an astonishingly realistic gas log fire, this is the focus of the main room.

My OXO sofa system occupies the centre of this space. Its seven interlocking pieces loosely define a conversational condition around the fireplace. Various examples of my Murano glass

designs for Salviati are around the room, mixed in with books and other objects. My favourite old pieces are an Etruscan cup I bought in the Mercato del Antiquariato in Arezzo. This sits well alongside two Roman objects, an oil lamp and a scent bottle. In the flat, I am looking for a sense of drifting and movement that works alongside a free attitude to function. I want to be able to choose between several places to sit, depending on the weather and the time of day. I like to have breakfast in the entrance hall, but work in the evening at the oval desk in one of the two bay windows. The apartment is a good place to entertain in, apart from the restrictions of the tiny kitchen, but it is also a good venue to hang out in *à deux*.

Then the whole place becomes a playground, a dressing room and a bedroom. The best moments occur when you discover a new place for a particular activity. And even after 30 years, I am still discovering what I can do where.

DISGUISES

The exhibition creates an artificial land-scape in which the Palladian models are positioned as they would have been in reality. BOPBAA have made an imaginary city of pedestals that place each building in its correct 'location' relative to the others along the Brenta valley.

ARCHITECT: **BOPBAA**   PROJECT: **PALLADIO EXHIBITION, SALÓ DEL TINELL, BARCELONA 1996**

Although Palladio may have been an important reference for the modernists and post-modernists alike, his enduring influence also inspires people like the architects in the group BOPBAA to experiment, as they have with this installation. After all, Palladio's work was sufficiently simplified compared with that of his classical contemporaries to inspire a conceptual interpretation. His unfolding spaces have an enduring fascination for architects today, whatever their stylistic leanings. This design is an example of how objects can usurp the identity of the original space.

Incongruously, this venue for the Palladian models is not a classical palace, but a fine vaulted room – part of a complex of buildings on the cusp between Gothic and Renaissance. As indicated first by the half-Palladian arch to the entrance, the design is an exercise in conversion. Though dignified and spacious, the exhibition space is by no means Palladian, but it has been cleverly converted to define an imaginary urban landscape.

Models of an identical scale, all made of the same material, sit on irregular grey plinths. You are encouraged to concentrate on the

unity of each individually lit architectural set piece. Though subtly dramatic, the darkness of the room works in direct contrast to the lighting directed onto the models. The room is toned down, and allowed to disperse its detail, giving the scale of the models the opportunity to take precedence.

The relationships between each of the models add further meaning. They are positioned to imply the real relationship between one building and another as they were originally actually built along the Brenta valley. The Villa Rotonda, in reality not far from

The monumental brick arches of the mid-fourteenth-century Saló del Tinell are subtly lit from below. The space is kept dark, with the only other accents of light falling on the models themselves. The dramatic effect of the vaults is minimized in favour of Palladio's buildings.

the city centre of Vicenza, is in the centre of the space. Other buildings built by the master are positioned in the exhibition as they are in the actual town. When you walk between them, you are in effect walking through artificial valleys carved out between the structures.

It is the impact of the overhead vaults themselves that finally reinforces the leap of the imagination. With each illuminated at the base, the edges of these arches define a series of abstracted arcs that draw the line of the night sky over the collection of architectural models. This approach adds a subliminal sense of context to the reading of the subject-matter; visitors to this many layered space need to develop the skill of tuning in to what is already there and making use of it.

Ahadu Abaineh's solution to the increasing number of people flooding into the cities of Ethiopia is to grow trees. He is in the process of planting groves of zigbas, which will eventually turn into 'shanty' towns in the sky. The ground floor of his prototypical tree house is lifted up from the ground, and large verandas blur the distinction between interior and exterior.

DESIGNER: **AHADU ABAINEH**   PROJECT: **TREE HOUSE, ADDIS ABABA**

There may not be much furniture in this house in a suburb near Addis Ababa, but here you wouldn't need it to accommodate all possible functions of eating and sleeping. In fact, it is the very emptiness of the spaces that seems a luxury. A piece of furniture itself, in the great living room of the forest, the Tree House proposes a way of living in harmony with nature in which the demarcation between inside and outside is literally blurred. Psychologically speaking, the Western obsession with the permanence of buildings is not always appropriate; in a country like

Ethiopia, permanence is less important than finding a place to live. With such a solution, the ingenuity of the architect has closed the circle between the primitive and the sophisticated. The structure of the Tree House is in fact part of nature itself, with four zigba trees defining its four corners. Although these trees are relatively thin, they are tall and straight, which means that the structural role of the elongated trunks does not interfere with the sprouts of leaves at the top, which continue to provide shade.

The house is designed so it can adapt to the life changes of the inhabitants. It is supported by four growing zigba trees on each corner, and infilled with untreated wood and flexible, easily altered materials. Mud has been used in a traditional fashion. This ecological solution reduces the consumption of environmentally unfriendly manufactured products.

The architect Ahadu Abaineh sees this design as a tangible solution to the housing problem in Addis Ababa. In Ethiopia, following a massive influx of people into the cities, most newcomers have to live in huts they have constructed themselves, where even the most basic living conditions are hard to maintain. Instead of opting for the usual environmentally destructive materials, such as concrete and steel, Abaineh has devised a system that reconnects the construction process to traditional ways of building, and ultimately to the landscape itself.

This first Tree House took only six weeks to build. Abaineh used untreated timber for the infill frame, and mud and pebbles to fill in the walls. The only manufactured materials are the corrugated iron and plastic used for the roof. Although wet weather is not that frequent, when it does rain the water drains towards the trees. Living so close to nature also has its hazards. Insects and furry creatures come and go as easily as you do, save for the raised ground floor that provides something of a barrier. Very large canopies mean that there is almost as much space on the

outside verandas as there is inside. The forest itself, so close to the building, is the biggest room of all.

One of the distinct advantages of the Tree House is that it can easily be altered and added to. Though you may not want to go above the existing three storeys, it would be easy to sequester the support of some of the surrounding trees. The fact that the nearby trees are not growing in a regular, orchard-like grid might add to the difficulties of setting out the structure, but the overall effect would enhance its organic spirit.

My Own Room Divided is a highly personal installation. Pellegrini divided a reconstruction of his flat, placing half in one truck and half in another. Through the open tailgates of the parked vehicles, glimpses of his life were offered to people in the night streets of Milan.

DESIGNER: **NICOLA PELLEGRINI**   PROJECT: **MY OWN ROOM DIVIDED, TRAVELLING INSTALLATION, MILAN**

PICTURES

Did architecture, or the art of the interior, invent the picture frame, and thus the picture? For a cave dweller, the cave's opening would have been a 'frame', a concept reflected in architecture by doors. You may want to depict the view of the outside on walls, like the Pompeians, or to represent it on wood, creating a picture framed by the limits of the wood. But pictures are not always flat. They can be three-dimensional, or you can live in one, with all the drama that this implies.

This is a room that has really travelled – Pellegrini's mobile installation toured the streets of Milan in two trucks. Occasionally they would park side by side to 'join' the room. More an art piece than a work pretending to be design, Pellegrini sets out to undermine preconceptions of what we expect a home to be. In the context of Milan, home is often an apartment that has been carved out of the traditional fabric of the city, but the scenarios that people create at home are based on personal needs. How well can these be shoe-horned into a building that was constructed for a com-

pletely different lifestyle? Most of the buildings in the historic centre were built for lives without electricity, let alone modern household gadgets, TV or the Internet.

Pellegrini recognizes the strength of these contradictions. He exposes the space in which he leads his life as though it were a living billboard, but one that is only perceivable at unpredictable moments. Its context is the daily life taking place on the streets. Performance art – similar in concept – has most frequently used the gallery as a safe haven from which to contemplate the differ-

ence between art and life itself. Rarely do such works take place in the city itself, but the itinerant nature of this piece means that Pellegrini exposes his private space to the much larger interior of the city streets. Throughout the performance, Pellegrini lived in the left-hand half, and videos of his childhood played on TV in the right-hand half. His recorded voice continuously asked the question 'Where are you going?' to reinforce the concept of home as a dynamically charged environment that matches your being much more than your sense of design.

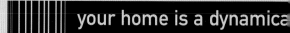
One truck was inhabited by Pellegrini, whilst in the other a television screen showed scenes from his childhood. His disembodied voice constantly demanded 'Where are you going?' In this instance, the interior symbolizes self.

As many people live on their own, the possibility increases for one-person homes to become ever more inscrutable. How many people do you think you know quite well, although you have never seen where they live? My Own Room Divided tells not just of the odd impressions that your own space might create if it were cut in two, but also the degree to which your private living space is hidden from the view of others.

Inevitably your home has a primary connection to who you are and how you live your life. Each one of us creates a three-dimen-sional portrait of ourselves through our choice of objects and the ways in which they relate to our lifestyles. Consciously or not, we all make various concessions to notions of style, which often con-tradict the need for personal comfort. Style offers an expression of broader values on a spectrum ranging from borrowing to inno-vative invention. Projects such as Pellegrini's are poignant reminders that the study of interiors is only meaningful if you look at inside spaces as dynamic sites, rather than as aesthetic tableaux or nice pictures.

PICTURES

By day, with doors closed, the four pods are inscrutable. But by night counter-weighted hinged canopies open upwards on power-assisted winch mechanisms to reveal a single-storeyed club room and a cocktail lounge, between a double-height function room and chill-out lounge.

ARCHITECT: **UNION NORTH**   PROJECT: **MPV NIGHTCLUB, LEEDS**

The most popular bars have rarely been 'designed' in the fullest sense of the word. Perhaps because the resources of bar owners are often too limited to accommodate designers, they have become good at creating atmosphere with a bare light bulb, a dominating sound system and a few camouflage nets. Designers know this, too, and often deliberately undermine flounce, keeping the venues simple and direct. One such project, the MPV nightclub by Union North, took its inspirational lead from the railway viaduct where it was to be located.

Union North have exploited the industrial context to the full. The result is a tangential set of interconnected interiors with a transgressive feel. Their site, a row of four arches, accommodates a chill-out lounge, club room, cocktail bar and function room for live music, comedy and food service.

The designers' creative process was intimately linked to the needs of realizing the four units, described by them as 'four chunky, toy-like pods, half troop-carrier, half handbag, emerging from their cocooning arches'. Since they are closed during the oop-carrier, half handbag, emerging from their cocooning arches

The units were constructed by a ship-building company as an upturned ship's hull, broken into 2 m (6ft 6 in) segments. The interiors use glossy laminate and lacquered fair-faced plywood which wraps around floor and ceiling in a single, unified membrane.

day, the effect of their front walls lifting upwards not only adds an extra sense of theatre to the otherwise industrial vocabulary, but also defines a frame that makes the interiors read like tableaux. Meanwhile, each outer shell, which is all moulded into one form, has a handle incorporated into it that says 'lift me up'. These capsules declare their readiness to be moved anywhere, though in reality they have been conceived to match the particular conditions of the railway arches and seem quite happy there.

If, as in these pictures, there are no people in each of the four

bars when you arrive, you peer into a sliced space that is stark enough to reveal all. But when the bars are full, and especially in the summer, the crowd becomes the performance, as it spills onto the cobbled road-surface outside.

Each pod has a symmetrical layout. The cocktail bar, for example, has the bar itself at the far end and two simple counters down each side wall. All of the pods have the same hose-down quality of the all-in-one bathroom pods in Japanese business hotels. Lighting is tucked in as though in an aircraft cabin.

The designers chose to work with local shipbuilders rather than with a conventional construction company. This helped achieve the rounded feel of the pods, and stressed their integration in the site. They also sought the 1960s aesthetic of the red moulded plastic found in early Olivetti typewriters or the grit bins familiar on the streets of Britain. The pods are deliberately modest and retro in spirit. The design is easy on the user. While inventive and practical, it solicits an alternative sense of ownership. They want the drinkers to be in charge.

The shop design was conceived as a stage. Clothes, light fittings and voiles hang from the industrial curtain track that runs across the ceiling. Like actors in a play by Chekhov or Ibsen, the dresses and mannequins inhabit the space.

DESIGNER: **BLACKSHEEPCREATIVES**   PROJECT: **VOYAGE FLAGSHIP STORE, LONDON**

In recent years, Conduit Street in London has become one of those sure-bet locations to open a shop. Vivienne Westwood first opened her doors here in 1990, and since then Issey Miyake, Mandarina Duck and Alexander McQueen have all taken advantage of the street's strategic location between Savile Row, Regent Street and Bond Street. Voyage is the most recent arrival, and to realize the design the company chose Blacksheepcreatives to invest the space with their brand of theatricality and makeshift chic. Like the clothes, which collage found fabric pieces together into skimpy little garments that look good on the dance-floor, the shop uses an assemblage of different materials and allusions to other kinds of space.

Viewed from the outside, it is clear that the cinema is on the list of references, with a movie-house board announcing the name of the shop. And this performance theme extends to the inside, though more in terms of movie studio than of the cinema itself. Making the most of a tight budget, but keen to get the house sense of luxury, the designers worked with materials selected for

their clichéd quality, such as plush wallpaper with traditional prints, mirrors and well-known pieces of furniture from the 1960s. Some walls are streaked with the remains of scraped-away paint. But the key to the atmosphere comes from a direct reference to the stage. The whole upper room is laced with an oversized curtain track, of a type standard in theatres. In a space this size, however, it has an overstated sense of mechanics and motion. This track has been cleverly used to work in all sorts of ways. It functions as clothing system, display and even as provider of

occasional curtains that, like the clothes, are made of fabric scraps sewn into voluptuous drapes. It also supports cute little light fittings made from lampshade frames with drops of crystal hanging from them.

For the customer, the whole space is rather like a giant wardrobe. You can brush through layers and layers of clothes, and there are some genuine antique wardrobes at key points around the room. In conjunction with the sense of faded grandeur and reclamation, you get the feeling that you are on the

The brief for Voyage was to reflect the
extravagant personalities of the clients.
The result is an eclectic mix of influences:
1960s furniture and wallpaper vie with
heritage-coloured distressed walls and
antique French wardrobes.

stage yourself. Though not as apparent to me as to the designers, the diagonal path across the space is meant to be a catwalk,
though its pragmatic function is to direct you towards the stairs.
Brushing past acres of velvet curtain, the experience of descend-
ing the stairs (to the hall of fitting rooms below) has its own
sense of drama and theatricality.

Housed in a former electrical warehouse 13,700 m (147,465 ft) square, the private club and hotel comprises 24 hotel rooms, a restaurant and lounge, three bars, a screening room, a library, spa and roof-top swimming pool. The original building materials were retained and act as a foil to the eclectic mix of modern furniture and vintage pieces.

DESIGNER: **ILSE CRAWFORD**   PROJECT: **SOHO HOUSE HOTEL, NEW YORK**

NESTS

The first time you hold a nest in your hand, you know that you have stolen something. Nests come from a different physical plane. Birds live in the air, and so does their architecture. They build their homes where we cannot reach them, in trees and on rooftops. Sometimes the human desire for distance from others compels you to build your own nest. This may not necessarily be in a tree – it could be behind walls and a closed door.

Sitting in the sixth-floor brasserie for breakfast, you gaze out across the shabby squat buildings of the Meat-packing District towards Tribeca and beyond to the remaining towers of the Wall Street financial district.

Though an extension of the club of the same name in London, Soho House, New York is quite different from its brother back home. Ex-style editor Ilse Crawford has used all her skills here to rework this urban scenario, contrasting a playful sense of nesting in the mansion with the hiss and grind of the streets below. She

has handled the interior with a knowing sense of comfort and luxury that relies on a European feel for patina. Bare brick walls, lumpy narrow plank floors and a bewildering array of textures and subtle colours combine to strike an offbeat escape from the world outside. There is a sense that your mad aunt, and not a corporation, has put this together.

Its aesthetics depend on proximity, material, texture and scale. With everything slightly staged and enlarged, grandeur and luxury abound. Chandeliers, worn leather chairs and collected objects sit with ease in the semi-industrial hardness of the warehouse building. Some of the floors are original narrow-strip hardwood, still buckled with age. The beams, incorporated as found and barely disguised, appear like those of traditional Parisian or Florentine grand spaces.

Since there is no grand staircase, the building works more as a discrete set of spaces, apart from the clues offered by the labelling on the oversized lift buttons (5th floor, library, cinema and rooms 12–9). The club occupies the whole of the sixth floor

The bedrooms vary in size and style, from Playground to Play House. Moroccan carpets contrast with concrete bathtubs, modern photomontages with *fin-de-siècle* headboards, and delicate chandeliers with heavily veneered woodwork and original industrial ceiling beams.

and is divided by glass partitions into a series of lounge bar and brasserie, so that you are unaware of the rooms below. More like the house in the film *Delicatessen*, the disconnection between spaces amplifies the fantasy. The manifold paradigm of the country house is more inferred than actual.

There may be no art as such, but there are innumerable provocations to play in this grown-up wonderland, an experience thought through with a sense of detail. My room, the Play House, has possibly the biggest bed (bar the Great Bed of Ware in London's Victoria & Albert Museum) that I have ever seen, let alone slept in. For my morning soak, I managed to over-froth the huge stone bowl of a bath at the bottom of my bed. What with games and sex manuals in the drawers, it is a shame I was there alone. Yet the atmosphere is a curiously familiar and poignant one, more the London you hold in your memory than Manhattan. Despite New York being 'new', much of its fascination in fact depends on its feeling worn in. Soho House is a rare acknowledgement of the spontaneity of the moment in an ambience of urban decay.

For this temporary installation at the Barcelona Hermès shop site, BOPBAA cleverly engineered a giant pivotal wall within the space. By day this moved back to allow the Kelly range of handbags to be displayed; by night it pushed forward to form a giant screen behind the façade on which various advertising images could be displayed.

ARCHITECT: BOPBAA **PROJECT: KELLY BAG INSTALLATION FOR HERMÈS STORE, BARCELONA**

This is strictly not a shop design, but more a temporary installation for Kelly Bags that used the shop space before the eventual project for Hermès was built. This gave the designers the chance to experiment with what a shop could do when it did not have to sell in the normal way. It only exists now as a series of photographs. From the start, the tiny location on the diagonal façade at a junction on the Barcelona grid had display potential. Its double-height, sectioned window could be treated as a single opening, and be made to shift its meaning according to the time of day.

Inside, the space of 50 sq m (538 sq ft) worked both as an interior and as a support to the façade. Most shops have to do both simultaneously, but BOPBAA decided to separate these conditions, and even to present different brands in association with each of them, as though inside and out were two distinct spaces that had little to do with each other. The two conditions also served to create a complementary set of opposed meanings. The designers wanted to emphasize the shop's multiplicity of purpose. When the space was open, they said, it was diurnal in

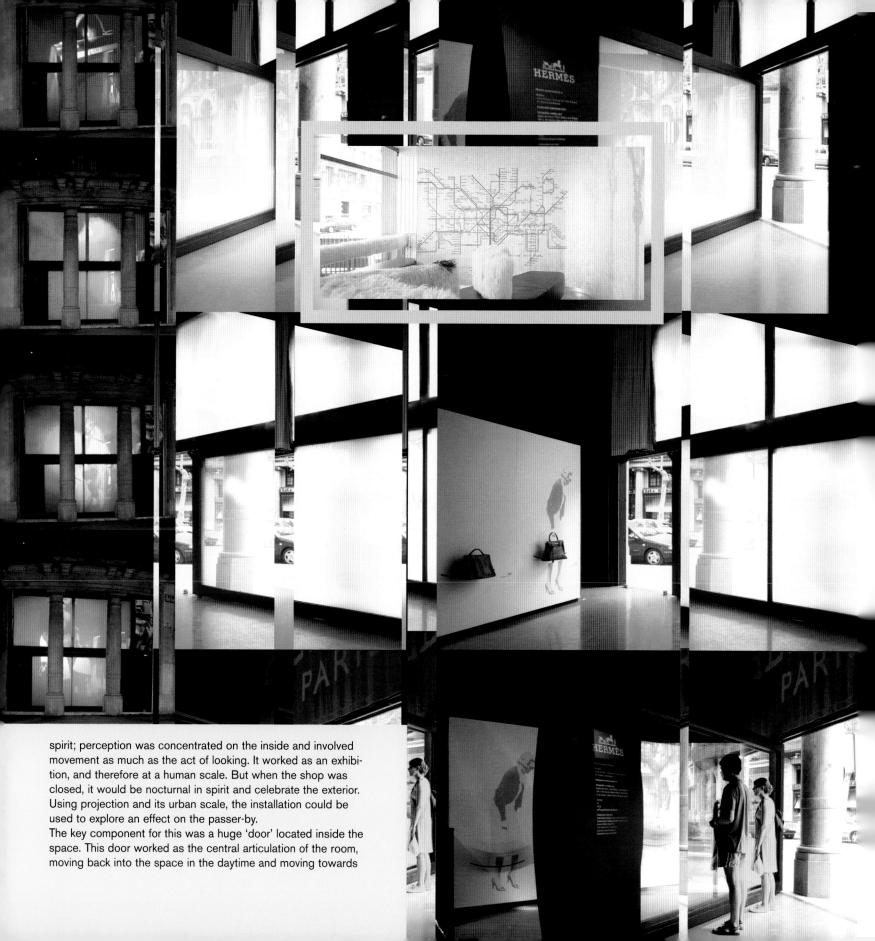

spirit; perception was concentrated on the inside and involved movement as much as the act of looking. It worked as an exhibition, and therefore at a human scale. But when the shop was closed, it would be nocturnal in spirit and celebrate the exterior. Using projection and its urban scale, the installation could be used to explore an effect on the passer-by.

The key component for this was a huge 'door' located inside the space. This door worked as the central articulation of the room, moving back into the space in the daytime and moving towards

The clear Kelly handbags were available for sale, but as they were covered in a translucent film of clear plastic, they took on the form of a giant sculptural wall. By night, a giant image of the Kelly Bag towers above the Barcelona street (right).

inside and out were t

HERMÈS

the window to become a screen at night. Each night the space was filled with smoke, and effectively the window became a single screen. Seen from the street, the film of Hermès products appeared in extra-large format. But inside, when the door was pushed back, the room provided a temporary exhibition space for clear Kelly bags, which people were invited to buy.

Crucial to these opposites were the two phenomena of scale and movement. It is unusual, to say the least, for a company such as Hermès to be so experimental with a shop that they intend to

refurbish. However, the event that this two-phase approach allowed did bring an art attitude into its space, if only for the duration of the show. Despite the fact that there was still a commercial undercurrent to this initiative, the way in which it communicated exploited the resonance of the interior as a pure space. With its mechanisms of transformation, it generated a conceptual discourse between architecture and the dynamics of the city.

The BasketBar is situated under the bleak yet imposing Van Unnick Building and was constructed as a subversive response to the institutional design of the university campus. Metaphorically, the weight of the tower behind has driven the Bar downwards below ground level, yet the basketball pitch towers upwards and acts as an icon of youthful energy.

DESIGNER: **NL ARCHITECTS**   PROJECT: **BASKETBAR, UNIVERSITY OF UTRECHT**

The BasketBar and its incorporated Skateboard Café bring a bit of street subversion into the institutional environment of the University of Utrecht. Since student housing became a possibility on the OMA-designed campus, where to go at night also became an issue, and this is NL Architects' response. The project reads the social needs of an otherwise orderly environment, and in its quirky way celebrates student-hood and the need to escape from the pressures of the classroom. Given the fact that the surrounding buildings are so large, this one plays with

belonging to the open space it sits in. Effectively, the lower level has been carved out from the ground, leaving the upper level, the basketball court, as not only a roof, but also an icon for the energy and ownership of the building.

The directness of the cage enclosing the court celebrates the box, but the visceral form of the skateboard hollow below marks a counter-icon that appears to burrow underneath it. This unlikely combination of fluidity and rigidity blows open the convention of inside and outside so that it is hard to define which is which.

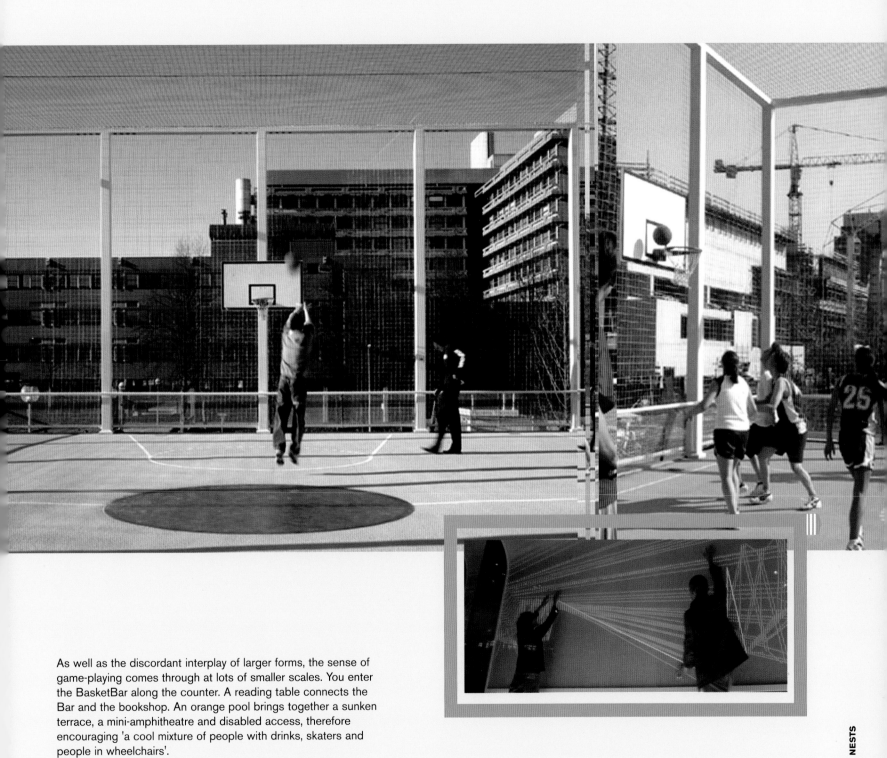

As well as the discordant interplay of larger forms, the sense of game-playing comes through at lots of smaller scales. You enter the BasketBar along the counter. A reading table connects the Bar and the bookshop. An orange pool brings together a sunken terrace, a mini-amphitheatre and disabled access, therefore encouraging 'a cool mixture of people with drinks, skaters and people in wheelchairs'.

As the Students Union wanted, this interplay of elements engages a huge range of activities, and brings new meaning to

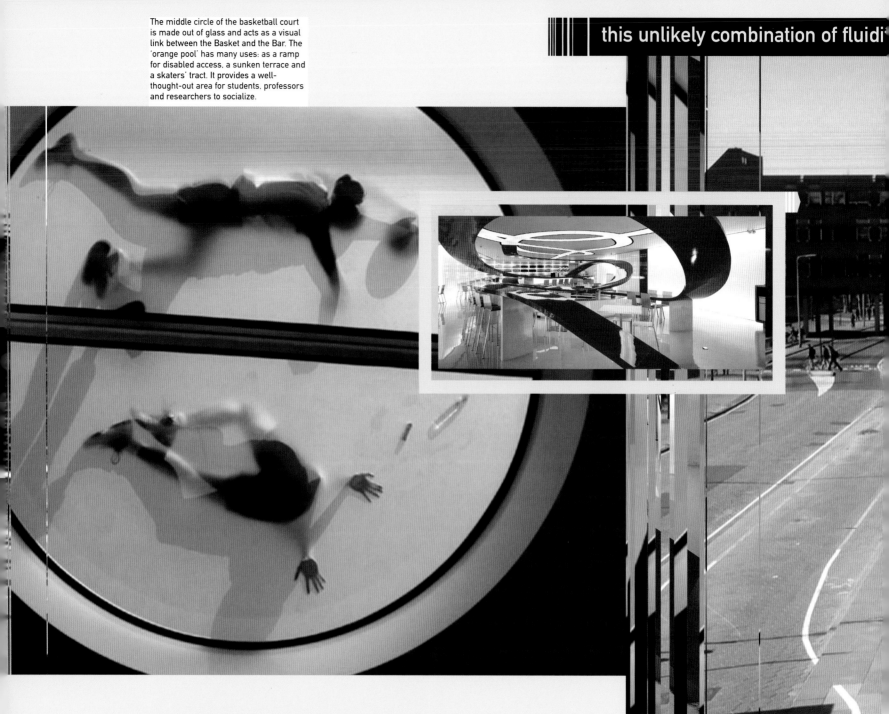

The middle circle of the basketball court is made out of glass and acts as a visual link between the Basket and the Bar. The 'orange pool' has many uses: as a ramp for disabled access, a sunken terrace and a skaters' tract. It provides a well-thought-out area for students, professors and researchers to socialize.

the term inclusive. The disabled ramp has not just been added as an afterthought, but built into the design.

There are so many optional activities suggested here but, apart from the basketball court, they are deliberately interconnected. Many elements suggest double usage. Most student bars concentrate on being friendly and, at best, design gets used as an aesthetic veneer to amuse, soften and legitimize the spaces. But this one takes activity as the lead. Whether you are skateboarding , drinking, reading or simply hanging out, the BasketBar might be for you. It encourages people to celebrate their roles, and to move beyond them. Upstairs, basketball players might be showing off, all the more because the middle circle of the court is covered with a clear glass panel so that people in the bar below can see the action up above them.

Marcel Wanders' Stone House clubhouse is part of Interpolis' Tilburg Headquarters. The ceilings were stripped bare and the cavernous overhead ductwork and dim lighting add to the night-time feel. It emphasizes the metaphor of the social gathering space, the pub, which Wanders has chosen in opposition to the alienating modular offices of the past. Inset is the meeting room – the Park House.

DESIGNER: **MARCEL WANDERS STUDIO**   PROJECT: **THE STONE HOUSE, INTERPOLIS HEADQUARTERS, TILBURG**

EGGS

Eggs represent the start of life. They offer a symbol both of rebirth and of the prototypical home for the unborn, protected by shells until the young creatures inside burst through. Fabergé encrusted eggs with jewels, and some architects have built ones large enough to accommodate rooms. Now, egged on by the possibilities of designing egg shapes with digital drawing programmes, designers are featuring them in more and more interiors.

Today no office is considered progressive unless it offers its workforce the levels of individuality and comfort that they would expect from a home environment. As an increasing number of personnel become nomadic, Interpolis, the Dutch insurance company, has proposed in its Tilburg Headquarters a viable and attractive solution with a distinctive 'feel-good factor'.

Active since the mid-1990s in conceptualizing an adaptable office, Interpolis invited leading Dutch designers Jurgen Bey, Piet Hein Eek, Irene Fortuyn, Joep van Lieshout, Ellen Sander Bas van

Tol, Marc Warning and Marcel Wanders to lend an unmistakable appearance to the latest in their office-wide programme of flexible working spaces. Distinctive styles allow employees to choose their workplaces. The so-called 'Tivoli' programme offers a 'cityscape' into which the workers can escape from their 'home bases' when they need a change of scenery. Under the director-ship of Kho Liang Le Associates, each member of the all-star team was allowed 500 sq m (1,640 sq ft) to demonstrate their creative potential, under the proviso that each 'clubhouse' had to contain not only individual workstations, but also a meeting room, a dining area and an area devoted to relaxation.

Marcel Wanders chose to keep each of the communal functions completely separate by housing them in 'caves', whilst the work-stations are in the open areas alongside. The Stone House draws upon the most obvious of social metaphors, the pub and park, as a response to the alienating and now antiquated idea of the standard office. The boulder-like forms loom out of their crepuscular setting. Wanders painted the ceiling and walls of the

The workstations lie outside the individual pods. The Park House (right) houses the meeting room and adds a splash of colour amongst the blacks and browns used throughout the space.

space either black or brown, covering exposed ventilation, lighting and pipes to evoke the atmosphere of being outside at night. The interiors of the caves shine out, welcoming users, and it is no surprise that this 'clubhouse' has become the favoured location of Interpolis' director, Kick van der Pol. The stones are built to strict stipulations of ergonomics, acoustics, audio-visual equipment, climate and lighting. All of the technological controls are individually regulated by touch-screen panels in each of the table-tops. An accent of frivolity comes in the form of the main meeting

room, the Park House, a single painted stone. 'It's like the girl with pink ribbons skipping through the park, the beam of sun, the nightingale in the dark,' says Wanders.

The drawback to this kind of 'communal individuality' is the loss of a personalized workspace. Lacking a place to display sentimental reminders of home and family, the employees at Interpolis have to find solace in physical self-expression, by affiliating themselves to an individual style that reflects their current mood.

The padded leatherette walls of the Sketch gallery (right) give way to a state-of-the-art projection system that runs around the entire room. Three projectors fire at each wall to stunning effect. The West Bar runs between the entrance and the gallery – here the walls gradually change from white to red. The 1970s-style furniture is given a facelift by the use of various black velvets.

DESIGNERS: **MOURAD MAZOUZ AND NOÉ DUCHAUFOUR-LAWRENCE**   PROJECT: **SKETCH, LONDON**

Between them, Mourad and Noé came up with a strategy that was sensitive to this historically loaded set of rooms and yet generated a contemporary sense of discovery. Though the Portland stone façade and cute swing card saying 'parlour open' belie the treasures inside, once you're past that daunting threshold you are truly in the world of Sketch. The designers have been sensitive in adding air and light to what would otherwise be overbearing grandeur. In fact, several of the plaster ceilings are Grade I listed and could not be touched.

A sense of drama and patina was combined with a digital ephemerality to create a series of rooms. While distinct from one another, they have the kind of flow you would expect from a gallery or a nightclub. Past a series of permanently installed art works that distort traditional furniture or open up panels of light within the walls, you hit the West Bar, and know that you have arrived. The white epoxy floor curls up to form the bar, but the colour on the walls changes gradually from white to red. At a high level, circular mirrors bend like heliotropes – their movement

magnified by the red lasers pointing at them – and deflect light around the room.

Next door, the enormous so-called gallery is a perfectly square space with all-white padded walls and a state-of-the-art projection system. Some twelve video projectors in 9/16 format can fill the room. With three projectors firing at each wall, together they make up a ring, achieving a stunning effect. Whatever is projected serves to transform and animate the space. A step further on you find the most extravagant lavatories this side of the Atlantic.

A reflection of one of the 12 egg pods in the East Bar unisex toilets. Each self-contained unit houses a WC and washbasin. The antitheses of these space-age conveniences are the lecture room toilets (right). Designed by glass artist Mehbs Yaqub, this 'jewellery box' uses bronze and copper glass panels embedded with Swarowski crystal.

A cluster of oversized eggs sits at the top of a double curving stair. Standing between these eggs, bathroom fittings that could easily have been original to the building contrast with the *Clockwork Orange* feel of the GRP ovoid cubicles.
Sketch has numerous other rooms, but those described here have enjoyed particular success, as they can be programmed differently through the day. Granted, the army of waiters who have to begin rebuilding and laying out the furniture in the Gallery every evening to make it ready for dinner must curse the design-er-owner pair. But all is ultimately worth it. Every night the Gallery restaurant is full, thanks to its style and inherent sexiness.
The West Bar has an exquisitely languid air about it, perhaps exceeding that of the New York bars of the 1920s that were its inspiration in the first place. In the post-9/11 era we may be super-conscious of security, but we certainly know how to flaunt our bodies, too. After all, eggs are not far removed from the mechanisms of sex – an association strengthened when you have to go back inside one to relieve yourself.

The display stands have not been designed for quick mass-consumption, but rather for savouring and enjoying the food on view. Future Systems have created a series of islands inspired by water droplets, emanating from the centrally placed escalators. The glossy white surfaces are deliberately neutral in order to emphasize the colour and variety of the merchandise.

CHEESE

DESIGNER: FUTURE SYSTEMS   **PROJECT: SELFRIDGES FOODHALL, MANCHESTER**

At one time the whole idea of the foodhall in a department store struggled to get past the notion of an old-fashioned grocery. Harrods foodhall has been on the tourist circuit for years. Its magnificent tiled walls and elaborate fish and meat displays succeed in creating an interior of culinary excess. Since then, stores such as Selfridges and Macy's have struggled to maintain this sense of excess while bowing to the shifting taste of their customers. But, working from inside the shopping experience, Future Systems have developed a completely new feel for their foodhall.

Selfridges' completely new store in Birmingham proved that a progressive building can inspire a broad base of customers. Its bubble-wrap façade has brought a progressive new identity to the city centre. The store has become a destination in its own right, providing a cosmopolitan set of experiences that simply did not previously exist. Their foodhall in Manchester works with similar ambitions. The designers wanted to develop the concept of a contemporary social focus for the new store. Food, they say, is where shopping begins.

A sculpted wall curves around the perimeter of the foodhall, displaying products to dramatic effect. The creatively exhibited selection of wines provides a dazzling backdrop to the bar (below). Moving away from the organic, the kitchenware displays, such as the Alessi stand (right), emphasize the man-made nature of their goods by using brightly coloured angular metal supports.

More specifically, this foodhall in Manchester is based on an observation of natural physics – of the ripple effect caused by a drop of water. Instead of the usual banks of shelves and fridges simply lifted from a catalogue, Future Systems have created a space with a fluid outer form, complemented by a circular series of displays and bars that appear to interact. Everything is clean, light and subtly shaped. Amid the escalators, the centrepiece of the floor is a fruit and vegetable display. The ripple effect generates the character of the display units, with refrigerated counters and eateries nearby. Everything is designed to have a soft, sculptural form. Various components in the hall combine in an overriding sense of breadth and lightness, and each of the display islands has been designed to suit the product. They mark out specific incidents in an open field of fluid circulation patterns. In a constant state of visual movement, the customer is given a refreshingly direct contact with the products.

Some of the displays, such as the table used for Alessi products, have a sparse simplicity. Goods on the asymmetrical glass table

are meant to 'jump' out towards the customers. In other places, the bewildering array of similar products has been used to make strong visual statements. Around the perimeter, a sinuously sculpted white wall displays a myriad of wines in a dramatic way, adding both scale and enclosure to the space as a whole.

Almost all of the furniture, products and textiles in Rashid's apartment are designed by his own hand. They form an 'evolving, on-going, dynamic gallery'. His work is displayed against a hard Cartesian white 'blank' gallery, enlivened by touches of fluorescent orange. The art work is by Rashid's wife Megan and by Christopher Wool.

DESIGNER: **KARIM RASHID**   PROJECT: **KARIM RASHID'S APARTMENT, NEW YORK**

STREAMS

Across the natural landscape, hills rise and valleys form. Together they collect moisture and then feed meandering, inspiring channels that flow according to gravity and topography. Although in conventional terms anti-architectural, flow is an essential quality of place, and can be incorporated into the lexicon of spatial definition. In an interior you might want to emphasize this aspect of human perception, and substitute solid architecture for movement and flow.

If you happen to be staying at the Maritime Hotel in New York, and your gaze falls on the building opposite, you are actually looking straight into the domestic world of Karim Rashid. This self-assured young man's career has focused on furniture design, spilling over into the world of interiors. Indeed, his apartment is almost entirely furnished with his own designs. Rashid relishes the opportunity to live the part expressed in his design: his privacy is his publicity.

He calls the apartment his 'Paraditic Lacuna' because of the

'non-stop, high-energy world' in which he lives. He has, in effect, turned his home into a promotional tool. It is a showroom that he happens to live in. Although he has not gone so far as to install a webcam, he does invite people to view his home on the Web. The design of the apartment began with the conversion of the original building from a stable into a clean box, with white walls and white epoxy floor. This relatively neutral container allows Rashid to circulate his latest pieces of furniture within the space. In the same way that the pure white of so many gallery spaces

pushes the art to the foreground, the emphasis here is on the furniture, as if it were art. Interior qualities are mostly defined by this furniture, and less by how Rashid has treated the enclosure. His style is languid and flirtatious. Much of the apartment is dedicated to the business of lounging and relaxing; most of the furniture is brightly coloured and voluptuously curvaceous. These pieces are located in the apartment in such a way that space flows around them. You step off the streaming movement zones into areas with specific function.

The kitchen is minimal, combining hard-faced, stainless-steel fittings with softer white plastic laminate cupboards. As Karim likes to entertain, this is the social hub of the apartment. He describes his 'Oh' chairs as the cheapest, most comfortable on the market.

Recently, Rashid has been test-driving his Omni sofa, a fuchsia creation intended to encourage orgiastic behaviour. Alongside, his Aalto-esque glass table forms the perfect plinth for some of his smaller products, such as candlesticks and vases.

As an alternative, Rashid and his family or friends may want to relax in the yellow zone – an assemblage of pieces with a 1950s inspiration. Both the pink coffee table and the sofas have those distinctively spindly, splaying metal legs. In the dining area, white is on overtime, and guests can sit on chairs designed by Rashid,

at a rectangular laminate table. Meanwhile the sleeping area has so much bedlinen that it almost cocoons the bed. Behind, a very large and somewhat architectural painting helps to place the sleeping area in the room.

A curved polyester, semi-transparent sheath runs around the *faux* walls of plywood that 24H have wrapped around the original masonry of the reception area in the Ashlee House Hostel. Classic images of London adorn this specially commissioned 'wallpaper', and a hatch opens into the reservation area. The banquette is covered in snake-print leather and fleece.

ARCHITECT: **24H ARCHITECTURE**   PROJECT: **ASHLEE HOUSE HOSTEL, LONDON**

Animated images of London life cover the walls of the reception of Ashlee House, a newly refurbished hostel in King's Cross. By day they welcome the itinerant youngsters who pass through the hostel's doors in search of a cheap bed, and by night they help to convert the space into a lively guest room that acts as advertisement for the hostelry. Large windows that give onto the street, and the clientele lounging and socializing on the custom-made, snake-print leather and fleece sofa, announce the fact that this is a hip place for young people to meet, talk and sleep.

Working on a very limited budget, the Rotterdam-based design company were given the task of transforming the reception from something you might expect to find in a downmarket ski resort to an environment more suited to an upmarket youth hostel. A new curved, plywood wall hides storage rooms, as well as office spaces. The service hatch of the reception desk opens out, but when closed is covered with the same 'wallpaper' as the rest of the room. Gone is the tatty notice board covered in tacky postcards, Underground maps and ideas of what to see in London,

replaced by murals that turn the walls into mines of living information. A half-transparent polyester mesh belt offers imagery of London, from the double-decker bus to bearskin-hatted soldiers. Henry Beck's floor-to-ceiling Underground-line diagram covers one wall and conceals a doorway into a room used for storing luggage. A foggy night-time scene is given extra impact by lanterns, which are cut out of the insert and illuminated by light bulbs, making the street lights appear surreal.

Artistic yet practical, this double skin avoided the expense of

The Internet room and the lounge offer further scenes of London life. The strong colours complement the pastels of the reception area, the main focus of the refurbishment.

dealing with the irregularities of the original walls or of adding new, customized light fittings. The interior of Ashlee House Hostel poses a new solution for a mobile, changing society. Cheap air fares have meant that many more young people can afford to travel, and they consequently require affordable, yet well-designed, accommodation. This simple idea proves that a limited budget need not result in a loss of quality, nor in the sacrifice of sensitive detailing.

Dwarfing everything in its path, Gehry's whirlwind of a sculpture emerges as a shaft from the basement and streaks across the ground floor of the Issey Miyake store in Tribeca. Kipping, who designed the interior, has linked both spaces by removing parts of the original wood plank flooring and inserting large elements of glass on the beams.

ARCHITECTS: **FRANK O. GEHRY (SCULPTURE); G TECTS LLC**

PROJECT: **ISSEY MIYAKE STORE AND HQ, NEW YORK**

Even if you're a casual admirer of Issey Miyake's clothes, you cannot help but be drawn into his shop on Hudson Street in Tribeca. The sensuality of the clothes is more than matched by the riotous stream flowing above the heads of the mannequins into the depths of the elongated reclaimed warehouse. This is Gehry working as sculptor of space, crossing the energy of sheer movement with the innate geometry of the building.

After Issey Miyake first visited Gehry's studio in Los Angeles, he described his vision of a Gehry 'tornado' whipping through the space, transforming everything in its path. This vision is matched by the outcome. The result is a fluid configuration of the warehouse building, dating from the late nineteenth century.

The sculpture itself emerges from a shaft that comes up from the cellar and then develops into a turbulent sprawl across the ceiling of the ground floor. It is made up from 1.3 x 2.4-m (4 x 8-ft) titanium panels, bent and attached to a contoured steel structure with Velcro pads. If you peer behind the panels, you can see four of these waving steel tubes attached to the ceiling structure and

The titanium panels are fixed to a steel armature with Velcro pads (below) and stairs lead to the downstairs display area. The atmosphere of this space is much more serene than that of the retail floor above. Glass walls and sliding doors house rolling racks which carry Issey Miyake's men's and women's collections, as well as the Pleats Please range.

a series of branches to which the titanium panels are attached. The effect of these is to combine sturdiness with a naturalistic sense of lightness and flow. Although large enough to compete with the architecture of the whole room, the scale also reaches out towards the clothes themselves.

The project was executed with the help of Gordon Kipping, an ex-teaching assistant and collaborator, who worked on the overall design. By removing parts of the original wood-plank flooring around the periphery of the space, it was possible to insert large elements of glass on top of the original beams. This has the effect of making the entire space seem to float and, visually, of connecting the ground floor with the basement level.

Kipping refined as many specific details as he possibly could, particularly the oversized stainless-steel wheels fitted to the clothing racks. Benches and tables are made from folded stainless steel sheet. These have an appropriate heaviness to balance the context of lightness suggested by Gehry's waving surface and the large areas of glass floor.

This is a far cry from Tokyo and the Japanese minimalist tradition. It acknowledges the way in which clothes form a visual yet intermediary interface with the world we live in. As a collaboration, it suggests that the interior does not need to be handled by one vision but can be the result of the intersection between several creative minds. That sense of collaboration extends to the fact that Gehry's son Alejandro was commissioned to execute two murals. They are inspired equally by the work of Miyake and of Gehry himself.

Glass etched with a wave pattern is used to separate a boardroom from the main space. Curtains can be drawn across for privacy in the reception area (right). The budget was tight and the practice responded by using cheap materials, such as PVC, mild steel, rubber and laminated MDF to playful effect.

ARCHITECT: **KATHRYN FINDLAY**   PROJECT: **CLAYDON HEELEY JONES MASON ADVERTISING AGENCY, LONDON**

RIBBONS

Instead of a wall meeting another at a convenient right angle, it might edge the room and bend into the next in a sensuous curve. Repeated many times and lifted from the ground, the wall forms a pennant or a ribbon. Apparently fortuitous meanderings, with shifts of direction and of surface, challenge the orthogonal. Since interiors are rarely direct enough to match surface with solid, they anticipate the surface breaking free and lifting into the room itself.

Unlike more prevalent efforts to define work space according to purpose, much recent thinking in interiors has been based on the question of how to link diverse spaces together and, as it were, to replace function with feeling. Drawing inspiration from choreography, landscape and the possibilities generated by digital modelling, many designers have been looking for motifs to link and connect individual areas.

Findlay's early works with her erstwhile partner Ushida are testimony to this trend. Projects such as the Truss-wall House and

the Soft and Hairy House in Tokyo configured these possibilities in complete architectural terms. Here at Claydon Heeley Jones Mason, Findlay has been confined to working on the interior, but she is no less ingenious with her solution.

As a leading advertising agency based in London, Claydon Heeley Jones Mason depends for its livelihood on wit and creativity, and these have provided the starting-point for Findlay's design. Creative teams need to feel good about working here, to be liberated rather than stifled by a corporate environment. The way people might relate to one another was of paramount importance, and the space needed to offer plenty of opportunity to drift from one area to another.

Findlay wanted the project to have a sense of flow that would override the traditional hierarchical uses of scale and material. She and the agency agreed on a way of organizing desks that works systematically, without appearing regimented. The spaces were to be playful and provocative, providing a stimulus to creative thought, as well as organized and comprehensible.

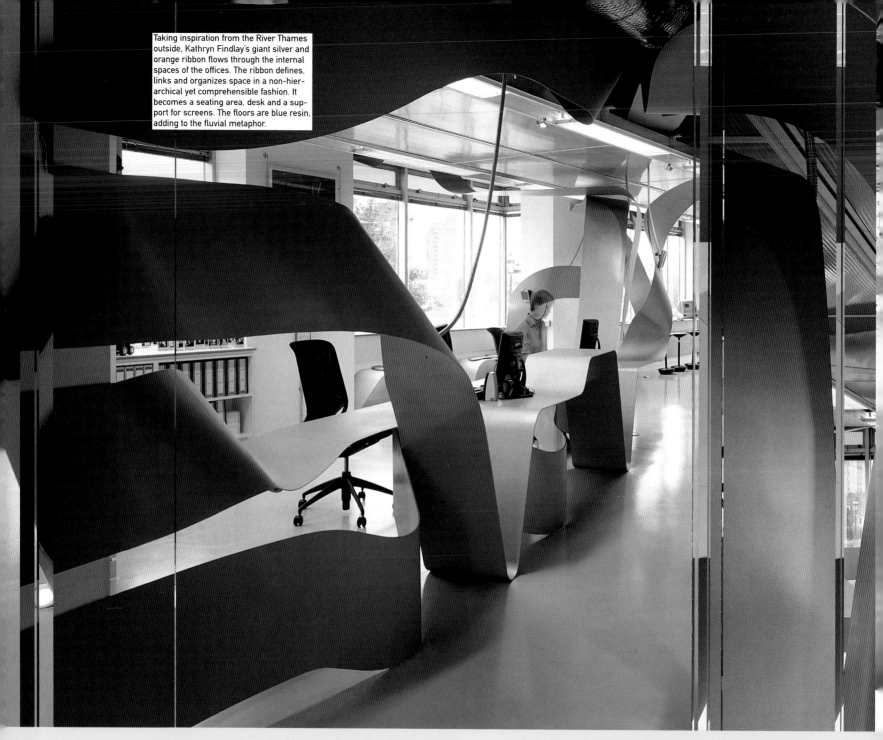

Taking inspiration from the River Thames outside, Kathryn Findlay's giant silver and orange ribbon flows through the internal spaces of the offices. The ribbon defines, links and organizes space in a non-hierarchical yet comprehensible fashion. It becomes a seating area, desk and a support for screens. The floors are blue resin, adding to the fluvial metaphor.

The design solution is appropriately open and unfinished. Since the building is situated adjacent to the River Thames, you don't need to look far to figure out where Findlay got her inspiration – the bends in the river. She has translated them into ribbons that transform their function as they travel through the whole height of the spaces. They lend ambiguity, continuity and change as they progress from one area to another. At one moment they are overhead, then they dip to the floor, then level out as a bench. Most of the ribbons are silver, reflecting the colour of the river water, but some are orange, the corporate colour of the agency. A light-blue resin floor adds to the sense of liquidity and openness. The reception, as the interface with the outside world, works as if it were a public space. This then fans out into more task-oriented spaces. As well as avoiding over-organization, working areas can grow and shrink according to the numbers in teams clustered around each client project. They occupy a grid that encourages change without allowing the inherent geometry to be apparent.

Novembre's long association with the mosaic manufacturer Bisazza is evident in the foyer of L'Una Hotel Vittoria, where a spiralling trail leads the visitor from entrance to reception desk. His communal seating system, 'And', was designed for Cappellini and is used here to promote interaction in the lounge. The doors to the bedrooms are individualized by life-size portraits copied from paintings in the nearby Uffizi Museum.

ARCHITECT: FABIO NOVEMBRE   **PROJECT: L'UNA HOTEL VITTORIA, FLORENCE**

Flamboyant designer Fabio has given design-conscious visitors a new destination in the very traditional setting of Florence. The hotel takes advantage of the fact that it is on the edge of the historic centre in San Frediano, one of the more popular quarters of the city. Although working within the limitations of an existing building, Fabio has used the relatively conventional exterior to emphasize the turbulent effects inside. When you enter you pass through a tumbling spiral of floral mosaic. Novembre is such a master of mosaic that you sometimes wonder if he has a financial interest in the material. He has realized that you can use it to combine the traditional imagery of decoration, such as that on fabric and carpet, with a digital twist. He designs the mosaic on a point-by-point basis, and makes it flow over curved surfaces. This entrance spiral joins together a number of diverse conditions. It forms a dynamic threshold, and as it progresses across the room it directs you forward to the reception, which it literally rises over, accentuating the lateral connections between this space and the bar to the left and restaurant to the right.

The private spaces are divided into bathroom, closet and bedroom, the bathroom being the first thing glimpsed when entering from the corridor. The bed (right) is raised on a platform. Square leather panels are surrounded by fibre-optic lighting. Colour-adjustable, this gives the feeling of sleeping within a jewelled box. Laminate cabinets are printed with images of garments.

Once you've checked in, your first stop will be your room, which you will find behind a repro painting on the door. Though identified by number, the experience is of a mysterious gallery of Old Master repros, somewhat incongruously offset by a wobbly, cloud-like installation on the ceiling. The rooms themselves are an odd cross between tomb and playground.
Cubic in every respect, the 'bedsits' are contained within a three-dimensional matrix of dark padding that has fibre-optic light points on the crossings. Strangest of all is the personal bar at the

foot of the bed. When you're up for a drink it works fine, but the effect from the bed is somewhat aggressive, especially since you're forced to watch the plasma TV over the top of it. The bathroom next door is almost as big as the rest of the room. It has the only 'his and her' showers I have ever experienced.

Downstairs the bar has more spirals – but this time in red upholstery. The idea is that tables and seats are incorporated into the form as it progresses through the space. This works to a degree, but you have the feeling you want to rough it up. Across the way

in the restaurant, the curving theme gets larger in a huge serpentine table designed by Atelier van Lieshout that occupies the centre of the room. A suspended stained-glass light follows it through the room, giving it a Las Vegas tilt. Though there are no one-armed bandits, there is a series of Internet screens around the periphery. You can sit and surf while having your breakfast.

A fibreglass ribbon trails through the building, delineating the intended circulation route through the store's shop, café, bookshop, florist and cosmetic department. In the café (below) it twists and turns, transforming into a spiralling bar and tables. Overhead, the dramatic effect is taken up in a curving light fixture (right).

DESIGNERS: **MASSIMILIANO AND DORIANA FUKSAS**   PROJECT: **EMPORIO ARMANI, CHATER ROAD, HONG KONG**

Armani's favourite architect, Claudio Silvestrin, designed the corpus of the five-storey building that makes up Armani, Chater Road in Hong Kong. However, it was his stylish friends the Fuksases who gave the new venture the breath of fresh air that it needed. Rather than insert twists and turns into the fabric of the building itself, they filled the spaces with swirls and spirals, as if inspired by the movements of the customers themselves.

Doriana says: 'At first we expected Giorgio to restrain our instinct to work with colour and movement, but he was behind us all the

way.' Colour is used with precision, and the result is certainly not some kind of Chinese fairground. Red is the Chinese colour for happiness, and frequently you see red ribbons spiralling through the streets. In the Emporio, spirals define both the approach to the café and the principal selling area.

The result is one of assertive elegance. Waving channels in the rock gypsum ceiling hide banks of spots, and at the same time carve out graphically choreographic lines that help to route the customer and the merchandise. The same can be said for the

Merchandise appears to float on glass shelves in glass boxes. The lights are invisible, placed above the ceiling and below the floor, and counters are magically raised from the ground. White walls and a blue-coloured epoxy resin floor with an iridescent water pattern complete the effect.

dipping table surface, which, in conjunction with the giant glass design of interlocking circles, makes a space that is layered, clean and animated all at once.

There is a particularly heightened wit in the treatment of the café (not unlike that of Novembre's bar at L'Una Hotel Vittoria). This swirling red plane goes wild once inside the seating area. From the horizontal it turns and lifts, and crosses itself, transforming from bar to tables along the way. And picking up on a detail from the waving wall inside the shop, it gets matched by a curving light strip on the ceiling. The doubling effect of the two together creates the impression of a space that has been cleaved open by some superhuman force.

Mariko Mori's Wave UFO installation has travelled from Bregenz in Austria to New York. It is illustrated here in the atrium of 590 Madison Avenue, home of the Public Art Fund. The 'space ship' – 5 x 11 x 5 m (16 x 36 x 16 ft) – was custom-built in a Turin automobile factory.

DESIGNER: **MARIKO MORI**   PROJECT: **WAVE UFO, TRAVELLING INSTALLATION, FIRST AT KUNSTHAUS, BREGENZ**

CLOUDS

The art of many churches in the Veneto and southern Germany sought to represent air. Gods were depicted perched on clouds, once considered stepping stones to heaven, peering down on us below. Now liberated from spiritual metaphors, clouds are linked rather to such commonplace experiences as flying. They still retain a mystery we can usually only dream of inhabiting, even though architects and designers are such good technicians that some really put us in the clouds.

It has been said of Mariko Mori, the Japanese artist, that she creates images of male fantasy from a woman's point of view. Wave UFO is no exception. Something like the oversized spherical TV that was such a design cliché in the 1960s, this giant eye is an object that invites you in to experience its retinal condition. Mori is inspired not only by oriental customs, traditions and religions, but also by Western culture, including fashion, science fiction and high-tech. Simultaneously, her work has an aesthetic purity and an in-your-face kitsch. Frequently, too, Mori's creations

rival architectural scale and, unlike conventional sculpture, offer the visitor the chance to experience them from within. From the outside, Wave UFO is very much an object, so much so that you know instantly that this is not the point. You might guess that its sheer weight will be the antithesis of whatever is on offer inside. When you enter the gallery, you cannot resist mounting those dinky little pad-like steps and slipping into the edgeless world inside. There you lie in carefully moulded recliners with light-up headrests, gazing at a swirl of coloured bubbles that

drifts overhead. Tardis-like, the expansive scale of the inside belies the weighty outer presence of the white plastic spacecraft. This work lies in a tradition of installations that transport you into artificial delirium – a substitute for the type of altered states that can be achieved through drugs. In Japan, where drugs are frowned upon, all kinds of similar experiences are on offer, from specially devised computer programs to watch at home to the more elaborate ones you can experience in clubs and bars. The capacity for an interior to induce this kind of altered state is noth-

CLOUDS

179

The stunning sculptural object is the latest in Mori's exploration of the relationship between the individual and the heavens. Three participants enter at a time. Once inside, computer graphics, brainwave technology, sound and state-of-the-art architectural engineering create a dynamic interactive experience conceived to link one person to another and to Mori's cosmic 'Nirvana'.

ing new. Even the ancient Egyptians, for whom the heavens were the greatest interior of them all, liked to decorate vaulted ceilings with stars. Relaxed enough to forget your body in the great lava lamp of Wave UFO, your mind will drift towards the outer limits and leave the ground behind.

Mori has a knack of grasping a nostalgic image that turns out to crystallize our efforts to connect with the cosmos. Yet the heightened experience of animated formlessness is still rooted in the highly codified parameters of everyday life. Wherever situated,

this fantastic creation will be something of an alien. Part natural condition, part artefact, Wave UFO is poised between our conflicting desires to relish and to escape from everyday reality. The work is designed to tour, journeying from gallery to gallery – in transit it splits into six parts, each in its own crate. When assembled, it is not strictly a cloud, at least from the outside; but inside, it is floaty enough to make you believe you are really flying.

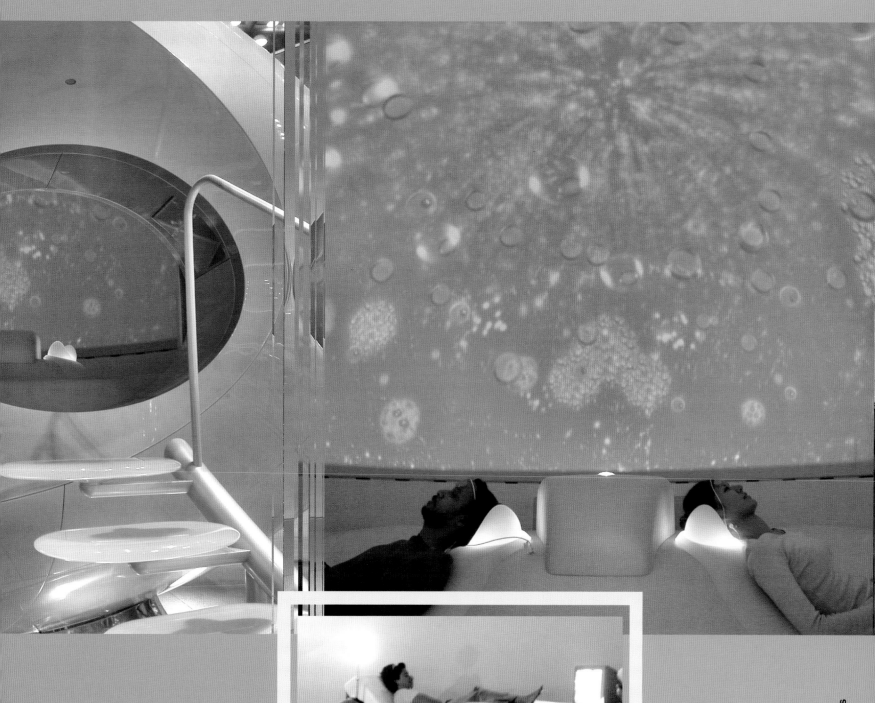

Blur is an intangible building of mist that emanates from 31,500 nozzles. Water is pulled up from the lake and a sophisticated computer system reads the shifting weather data, interpreting the information and regulating the water pressure accordingly. The resultant vapour is unpredictable, yet follows certain tendencies in height and density, according to current climatic conditions and the temperature of the water in the lake.

ARCHITECT: **DILLER + SCOFIDIO** PROJECT: **BLUR BUILDING**, **LAKE NEUCHATEL, YVERDON-LES-BAINS, SWISS EXPO 2002**

Since this project has no walls, you may think it a perverse inclusion in a book about interiors. But this is exactly the kind of issue that this project intends to raise. When you are in the heart of it, you are very much inside a cloud, truly enveloped within it. Sound is muffled and your vision is restricted to a few feet in front of you, yet the sensation is comparable to being inside some large and conventional architectural space. This is quite an achievement for a structure that, while it has floors and stairs, has no solid walls.

Though technically difficult to accomplish, the actual concept was relatively simple. A basket-like steel structure, over 100 m (328 ft) across, housed ramps and two platforms. Water from Lake Neuchatel was constantly drawn up and blasted as a mist through thousands of tiny jets, placed at regular intervals along each tube. These composed the distribution web that wrapped and infiltrated the structure. Once inside, you could pass from inside to out with remarkable ease, like diving through a mythical mirror as though it were nothing more solid than air.

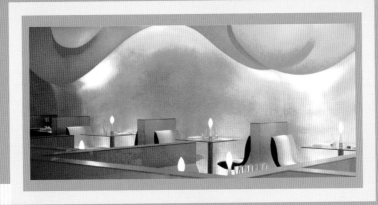

This 'architecture of atmosphere' is reached across a bridge. Once inside, all visual and acoustic references are erased; the visitor enters a non-space of 'white-out' and 'white noise'.

From the land, the swirling mist appears to have the natural dynamism of a real cloud. Though the source of the vapour was fixed, wind and air pressure dragged it outwards or upwards, depending on the weather conditions. On an average day, the cloud would amass around the structure, to the extent that no part of the platform was visible, while any wind stretched the vapour out across the surface of the lake. You just saw little tented figures disappearing into the mist and occasionally popping up above its top level, as if walking on air.

You could only see the Blur pavilion when you had entered the Swiss Expo compound, where it was the main focus of the site. Eventually, you followed other visitors into the cloud. Before entering, everyone was offered a waterproof mac, not only to keep clothes dry when surrounded by water and mist, but also to prepare you for a powerful, intimate experience.

Although Diller + Scofidio are architects by training, much of their work is executed in a gallery context. They delight in demonstrating the ambiguity of architectural phenomena, and Blur is no

exception. They observe that 'unlike entering a space, entering Blur is like stepping into a habitable medium, one that is formless, featureless, depthless, scaleless, massless, surfaceless and dimensionless. On the platform, movement is unregulated and the public is free to wander in an immersive acoustic environment.' Though they add that 'there is little to see' from within, I disagree. All the senses, especially vision, become very acute, precisely because you can only make out the vague forms of other people. You are witnessing a mental condition.

CLOUDS

Bloomberg uses architecture and design in all its offices to raise its public profile. In their showcase space, just in front of Tokyo Central Station, the public is invited to play with stock data in a very tangible way. Giant LED screens hang from the ceiling, resembling icicles – hence the project's name, ICE, which also stands for Interactive Communication Experience.

ARCHITECT: **KLEIN DYTHAM ARCHITECTURE**   PROJECT: **BLOOMBERG ICE, TOKYO**

If you are a busy Tokyo commuter with some spare time before your train is due to leave, you may well be tempted by Klein Dytham's cloud, an interactive wall just in front of Tokyo Central Station. Commissioned by Bloomberg, the international business TV channel, the idea was to give business TV a more youthful angle and to attract an audience otherwise puzzled by the streaming data of Bloomberg's normal screen format.

Like many Japanese cities, Tokyo has extensive networks of covered streets, especially around such stations as Ueno, Shibuya and Shinjuku. Tokyo Central at Maruonuchi is no exception. Larger outdoor spaces have the character of rooms defined almost exclusively by advertising and giant TV screens. All that is missing are the sofas and the drinks cabinet. This installation plays on this condition of the virtual outdoor room. Although not strictly an interior, it is contained by a wall of glass; but the ICE wall reads more like an animated billboard than a room. But because it is interactive, people also make it their own. The effect is to turn the entire proximity into a dynamic public space.

Measuring some 5 by 3.5 m (16ft by 11ft 6 in), this digital wall translates financial news and data into a playful, dynamic image that is triggered by the user. When you stand within half a metre of the surface, it detects your presence and responds to your movements. When no one is near, it displays stock information rising or falling in simple graphics but whenever a punter approaches, a menu drops down, offering four possibilities of games to play: a digital harp, a digital shadow, a digital wave and digital volleyball.

Together these add a deliberately unrelated set of play possibilities to the ubiquitous data 'weather system' of the financial markets. Each one of these games responds continuously to your movement and temporarily serves to obliterate the data display mode. As a player, you have the chance to affect the wall totally, and consequently to change the space all around it. The fact that it is enclosed by a glass wall ensures that you have a temporary sense of intimacy and control, even as you perform an otherwise public demonstration of skill.

This is one of the first of what will have enormous implications for public space in the future, and for the ways in which advertising and culture can combine. While in Europe public space is often institutional in character, many crossings in Japan become public spaces through the entertaining role of advertising. The ICE wall, however, brings the advertising media down to the level of the street. Its action is experienced so close up that it defines itself according to the identity of the user.

CLOUDS

Illustrating the hyper-urbanism of New York, Hong Kong and Tokyo, Rashid data-mapped the skyscrapers of these individual cities. Influenced by the way that a car's shiny, reflective body picks up and distorts the buildings it passes, he used large, suspended forms derived from auto-mobile tectonics on which to project the resulting digitalized images.

ARCHITECT: **ASYMPTOTE**   PROJECT: **FLUXSPACE 3.0-MSCAPE INSTALLATION FOR DOCUMENTA XI, KASSEL 2002**

MOVIES

The power of story-telling, of narrative, underlies all our actions, however unconscious or apparently straightforward – and every room tells a story. Movies take this further, providing a mainstay for the creation of rooms. No wonder, with the expectations movies arouse of extreme passion and violence, with the suspension of disbelief, that designers want to transfer this spirit to rooms. We long to live on the other side, as characters in our own continuous performance.

Many movies include sequenced driving through city streets, and through the windscreen show the stream of buildings passing on either side. As opposed to conventional images of buildings, this stereotypical experience condenses the city in question as if experienced through your eyes.

Imagine, too, that as this car is passing along those streets its shiny surface is catching and reflecting that same stream of images – as though the city was attracted to the moving object. It is this characteristic of the car as 'attractor' that fascinated

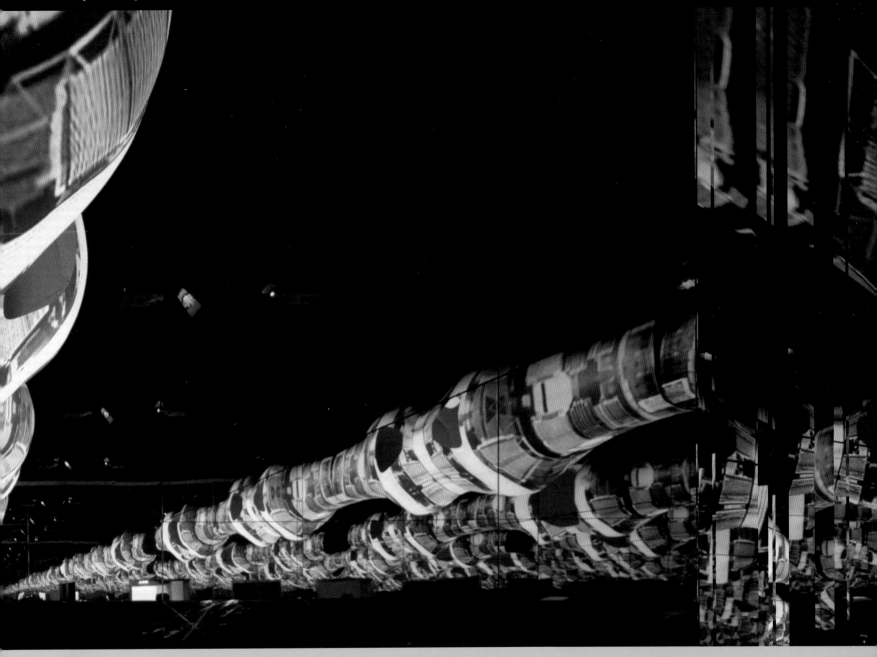

Hani Rashid enough for him to use the phenomenon for his installation at Documenta XI in Kassel, Germany.

Rashid has always been drawn to the concept of the city as a dynamic interior, and this project translates the idea into a new type of visual experience. He began the process by working with the car body. All cars have a surface that consists of a complex combination of convex and concave curves, and naturally these serve to distort the reflections that fall on them. Rather than plumping for any one particular car, he developed a digital abstraction that represented all car bodies. The generic car surface that resulted formed a central object in the installation, and was used as a surface on which to project other images.

With the aim of translating hyper-urbanism, Rashid also spent some time data-mapping the façades of buildings in several quintessentially big cities: New York, Hong Kong and Tokyo. From these he constructed an infinite environment of digital data to become his Mscapes. He then added recordings of people in conversation, and attached these to images of specific skyscrap-

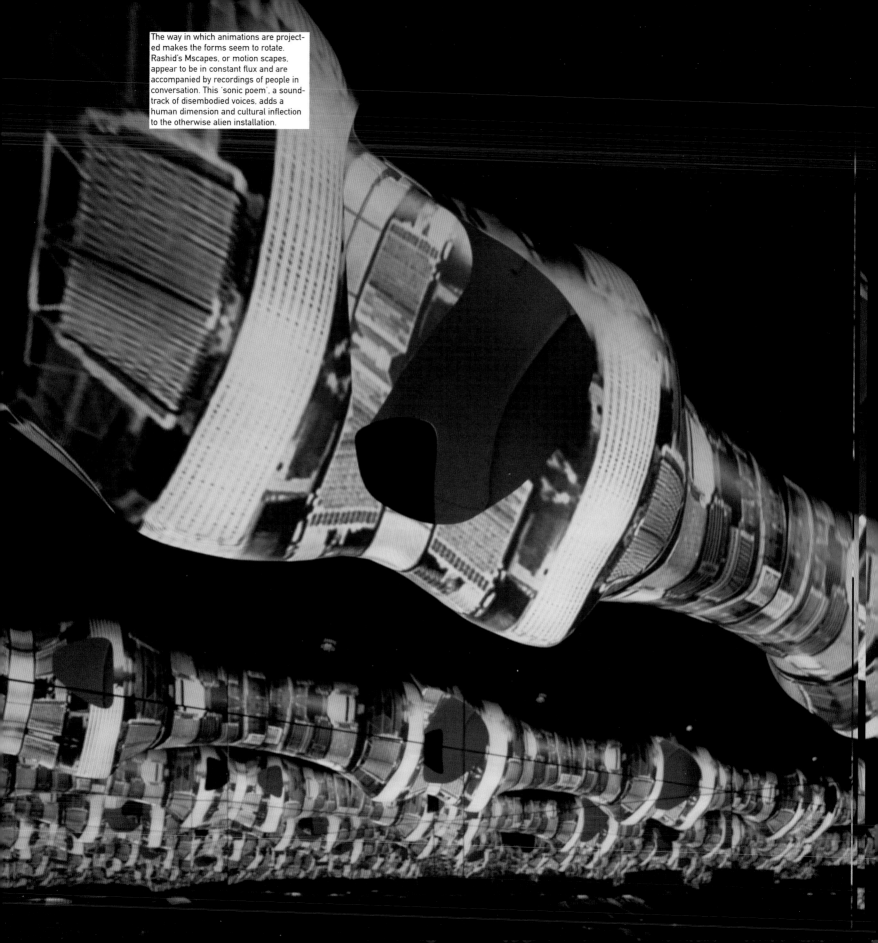

The way in which animations are projected makes the forms seem to rotate. Rashid's Mscapes, or motion scapes, appear to be in constant flux and are accompanied by recordings of people in conversation. This 'sonic poem', a soundtrack of disembodied voices, adds a human dimension and cultural inflection to the otherwise alien installation.

ers. Each one of these images tracks along the length of the building, and when projected appears to be a wheel rather than a part of a façade.

These animations were then assembled and projected onto a car body shape, a solid form 4.5 m (15 ft) long. The net effect of the animations was to make the form itself appear to be rotating. Each of the buildings and its attached soundtrack thus became a rotating slice on the surface of the suspended shape. The installation, which Rashid calls FluxSpace 3.0, is both multi-sensory and powerfully transcends any normal boundaries of scale. The final result constitutes both an interior itself and one that represents the enclosure of the city through its condition as data. As a complete, mesmeric installation, FluxSpace 3.0 reveals the DNA of the contemporary urban condition.

Slicing through black wood walls and resin floors, a grid of red, green and blue neon light boxes pulses and alternates in sync with the music. Depending on the crowd, the colours are combined to create varying ambiences. Young Paulistas dance as if suspended in a futuristic void of light and sound.

ARCHITECT: **MUTI RANDOLPH**   PROJECT: **D-EDGE NIGHTCLUB**, **SÃO PAULO**

In São Paulo, all fired up with nowhere to go? Head down to the D-Edge, a club that suspends you and up to 800 of your fellow revellers in a matrix of pulsating light. Rio-based graphic designer Muti Randolph wanted to expand his lifelong passion for computer games into a club setting. As a graphic and set designer, he is used to seeing his work on screen translating into the sets for music videos, but the commission to design D-Edge, from club owner and DJ Renato Ratier, gave him the chance to apply his skills to a real space. He used a simple orthogonal installation of

lighting strips in the walls, floor and ceiling to generate a series of black spaces that vibrate with a sense of movement.

This environment exploits geometry to delirious effect by linking the lighting system to the sound. The three-dimensional grid of light operates as an analogue of a computer monitor, linked to the music so that it is the room, not the screen, that translates the sound into a visual condition. Each light strip incorporates red, green and blue light so that it can pulse and change colour according to the instruction from the command computer. This

The bar area is enlivened by the same light show, although reduced to a less frenetic level. Muti Randolph freely confesses his obsessions with computers and video games, which inspired the design of the nightclub. The grid of light and the dark background are an analogue for the computer monitor.

produces flickering light that facilitates the movie-effect movement. Add to this the possibility of pre-selecting the colour, and you have a dynamic system that can adapt to the mood of the music and the crowd on each successive night.

Here the style élite of São Paulo can escape the brightness of the beach to flaunt their lithe bodies in more subtle ways in this erotically charged environment. Naturally, the most frenetic effect is reserved for the dance-floor, where the fashion for black adds further to the sense of dynamism and suspension. Faces and

limbs caught in the visual crossfire distance the sight of any of the crowd into fragments, as if caught on film.

Normally you would expect the impression to be accompanied by dissolving forms and sensual curves, but Randolph has gone the other way. He has exploited the matrix surrounding you. As a dancer, you are suspended, to the point that physical space dematerializes. Everything apart from the lights is black, including the wooden walls and the ceiling, which otherwise has a perfunctory feel. The lights on the ceiling have in fact something of the

suspended fluorescent about them, or at least they would if they were in a factory or cheap office space. The hard and shiny resin floor serves to multiply the right-angled arrangement of the lighting strips, so that, when in fully charged mode, this apparently rational system produces a sublime sense of disorder that fuses time and space.

And if it all gets too much, you can always relax in the bar next door – the décor is the same, but the pulsing a little calmer.

DESIGNER: **SHELL WITH THE RENEWABLE ENERGY SYSTEMS (RES)**   PROJECT: **SHELL ELECTRIC STORM, LONDON 2003–04**

If you've ever seen those huge arc lamps blasting light into the
windows of houses, you know that it is not that difficult to reproduce weather conditions on film. Movies rely on plausibility, but
you enjoy the fact that they are fictional, and the same is true for
much of the city. There are modern versions of public space
design that exploit this sense of movie-making.

Now we are more inspired than ever by the intrusion of nature
itself into the predominantly artificial urban environment. In Japan,
walking through rain is thought to be romantic, while in Britain it

is more likely to be considered a nuisance. On the other hand,
mist has some of the Japanese connotations. Add colour to this
scenario and you might be in the Shell Electric Storm, a project
that brought a movie-like artificial weather system to the South
Bank in London.

If during the winter months of 2003 you were to drift after dark
across the newly built west side of Hungerford footbridge, you
would have been surprised to see a coloured cloud. This scene
occupied the middle of one of the widest panoramas across

Jonathan Porritt, chairman of the UK Sustainable Development Commission, could well have had this installation in mind when he made the controversial comment that wind turbines were 'objects of compelling beauty'. At night, the South Bank became a theatrical stage set of colour and light. Shrouded in a magical mist, visitors strolled to the mesmerizing hum of the giant revolving blades above.

London – the wide-angled view of the London Eye, County Hall and the Palace of Westminster.

For a three-month period, this artificial weather system of light, mist and sound brought an ever-changing sense of enclosure to the river walk. Poking upwards through the mist was a single, fully operational offshore windmill capable of generating up to 225 KW, enough to match the power drawn from the national grid for the whole installation. Rising 43 m (141 ft) above the river walk, its scale became apparent against the backdrop of the

Shell Building. The turbine was intended to draw attention to Britain's efforts to harness offshore wind to fulfil energy needs. Over a distance of half a kilometre (a third of a mile), the installation incorporated 40 trees along the promenade on either side of the bridge. They were divided into ten groups, each with its own co-ordinating switching mechanisms. Each individual tree was harnessed with mist jets, lighting bars and speakers, all of which altered their emissions according to data gathered from atmospheric conditions, including tide levels, temperature and humidity.

The lighting bars were installed at two levels within them. In operation, the diffused effects of the light penetrated the full depth of the mist. Ambient and sharp hot spots added a further variety of effects in this dynamic network.

The two tree lines on either side of the promenade were used as boundaries of an open architectural structure to define a loose kind of urban interior. Although powerful enough when viewed across the river, the most magical way to see them was from the inside, where you could enact your own urban love story.

PROJECT CREDITS

BODIES

Ichthus Business Centre, Rotterdam, The Netherlands
Architect: 24H Architecture
Project team: Maartje Lammers, Boris Zeisser (Principals); Jeroen ter Haar, Severine Kas, Sabrina Kers, Gerben Vos, Heleen Bothof
Client: Ichthus Hogeschool
Van Gils projecten; de Jager Meubel – en interieurbouw; Vertical Vision Furniture, PuzzleSIT; 24H Architecture – Maartje Lammers, Boris Zeisser

Sportopia, XXV São Paulo Bienal, Brazil
Designers: Atelier van Lieshout
Client: Mondrian Foundation

Mandarina Duck Store, London, UK
Interior design: Marcel Wanders Studio
Project architect: Harper Mackay
Client: Mandarina Duck
Main contractor: Kingly
Lighting consultant: Modular Lighting
Mannequins, Gulliver, free-standing mirrors: The Set Company
Glass displays: Studio LB
Floor finishes: Escopalatino; Desso
Wall finishes: Tyvek, DuPont
Multiple(x) lighting: Modular Lighting NL

WOMBS

Carlos Miele Flagship Store, New York, USA
Architect: Asymptote.
Project team: Hani Rashid, Lise Anne Couture (Principals); Jill Leckner (Project architect); Noboru Ota, John Cleater, Peter Horner, Cathy Jones (Project team); Michael Levy Bajar, Janghwan Cheon, Teresa Cheung, Mary Ellen Cooper, Shinichiro Himematsu, Michael Huang, Lamia Jallad, Ana Sa, Markus Schnierle, Yasmin Shahamiri.
Client: Carlos Miele
Engineers: Kam Chiu (PE)
Lighting design: Focus Lighting Inc
A/V consultant: Ben Greenfield
Contractor: Vanguard Construction & Development
Fabricator: 555 International

J-Pop Café, Odaiba, Tokyo, Japan
Architect: Fantastic Design
Project team: Katsunori Suzuki and the Fantastic Design team
Client: J-Pop Café
General contractor: Circus Inc.
Chairs: Oh Chairs by Karim Rashid for Ombra; Panton Chairs by Werner Panton for Vitra; Soft Egg Chairs by Philippe Starck for Driade
Computer-controlled LED lighting: Color Kinetics Japan Inc

Bathroom Exhibition for Alessi, Milan Furniture Fair 2002, Italy
Design concept: Stefano Giovannoni
Client: Alessi SpA
Bathroom furniture: Alessi SpA
Installation: Eurostands
Lighting: Pollice Illuminations

PLAYPENS

The Start Room, Tate Modern, London, UK
Designer: FAT
Client: Tate Modern
Contractor: KO Creations
Painting/sign writing subcontractor: Castleford Signs

Fisherking Developments Headquarters, Winchester Wharf, London, UK
Architect: Softroom
Project team: Christopher Bagot, Daniel Evans, Steven Cox.
Client: Fisherking
Contractor: Lad Construction

2A Garner Street, London, UK
Architect: FAT
Project team: Sean Griffiths, Sam Jacob, Charles Holland, Dmitrij Kudin, Laura Cramwinkel, Mie Olise, Sacha Leong, Deborah Reis
Client: Lynn Kinnear
Contractor: Blake Builders
Quantity surveyor: Andrew Turner and Company
Structural engineers: Elliott Wood Partnership
Daylight surveyor: Schatunowski Brooks
Suppliers: Eternit Weather Board 50 (external weather boarding); MT Architectural Aluminium (aluminium windows); Fendor Hansen (fire-proof steel windows); McKenzie-Martin Ltd (roof lights); Alco Beldan Ltd (sliding aluminium doors); Lyncrete Burkle Services Ltd. (precast concrete stairs); Thermalite (concrete blocks); Mister Resistor (light fittings); Steelrad and Hudevad (radiators)

TABLES

Menswear Department, Selfridges, Manchester, UK
Architects: Softroom
Project team: Christopher Bagot, Steven Cox, Cornelia Fischer
Client: Selfridges & Co
Contractor: PBH Shopfitters.
Structural engineer: Techniker
M&E: Oscar Faber
Quantity surveyor: Boydens & Co

Morimoto, Philadelphia, USA
Architect: Karim Rashid
Project team: Karim Rashid (Principal); Jalan Sahba (Space Director and Project Manager); Lisa Rusakova (Architect)
Client: Starr Restaurant Organization
Lighting: Focus Lighting
Curtain wall: Paul Rabinowitz Glass Company
Booth and sushi-bar seating: Galerkin Design
Lobby seating and lounge ottomans: Nienkamper
Glass tables: Curvet, USA
'Candle' table light: Karim Rashid

Private City/Public Home, Dutch Pavilion, Biennale 2000, Venice, Italy
Pavilion design: NL Architects and Bernd Druffel
Client: Ministry of Education, Culture and Sciences and in collaboration with the Netherlands Fund for Architecture
Commissioner: Kristin Feireiss
Video installation: One Architecture and Elisabeth Dijkstra
Film: Anna Abrahams and Jan Frederik Groot, Rongwrong Foundation
Furniture design: Dumoffice, Optic, Jacobina Tinnemans
NL lounge Magazine De-Fence: Rianne Makkink, Herman Verkerk, Jop van Bennekom
NL lounge website: Just Schimmelpenninck
Multimedia consultant: Willem van Weelden
Lounge-keeping: Various artists and students from the Netherlands Architecture Institute
Coordinator: Angela van der Heijden
Project team: Angelo Grasso, Sarah van der Pijl
Communications: Angeli Poulssen
Production: Rob van Leeuwen, Herman van Dongen, Godard van Randwijck, Roderick Guèpin

SHEETS

'All in One' laminate design for 'DigitalPrint: A New Generation of Surfaces' Exhibition, Milan Furniture Fair, 2003, Italy
Designer: El Ultimo Grito
Client: Abet Laminati
Exhibition curator: Paola Navone

DIA Center for the Arts, Chelsea, New York, USA
Architect: Jorge Pardo
Client: Dia Center for the Arts
Furnishings: Alvar Aalto, Marcel Breur, Nick Dine
Clay model of VW Beetle: Volkswagen

Courrèges Headquarters, Paris, France
Architect: André and Coqueline Courrèges
Collaborating architect: Jean Bottineau

BOXES

Tendenza Discothèque, Monteriggioni, Italy
Architect: Stefano Giovannoni
Client: Michele Monticini
Installations: Eurostands
Lighting installations: Johanna Grawunder

The Bohen Foundation, New York, USA
Architect: LOT/EK
Project team: Ada Tolla, Giuseppe Lignano, Maggie Peng
Client: The Bohen Foundation
General contractor: IBK Construction
Consulting engineer: Ove Arup and Partners Consulting Engineers PC
Container supplier: Sea Box Inc
Container fabrication: United Artists Federation (UAF)
Resin/rubber fabrication: Jan Hilmer
Wall panel track system: PDO Inc

Win a Cow Free Store, Tokyo, Japan
Concept design and client: Setsumasa Kobashi
Construction: D-BRAIN

SCRAPS

Free-state AVL-Ville Raft, Swiss Expo 2002, Biel, Switzerland
Architect: Atelier Van Lieshout

BSBbis (Beursschouwburg), Brussels, Belgium
Architects: B-architecten bvba in collaboration with DHP-architecten bvba
Project team: Evert Crols, Dirk Engelen, Sven Grooten, Annemie Bosmans, Kris Blykers
Client: Ministerie van de Vlaamse Gemeenschap, afdeling gebouwen
Structural engineer: ABT/Lipski nv
Special techniques: ABT/Lipski nv
Acoustical engineer: Pujes, Spruytte & Associates eesv
Theatre technique: TTAS
Landscape architect: Juurlink en Geluk bns bv

Broome Street Loft Conversion, New York, USA
Architect: Block Architecture
Project team: Zoe Smith (Project Architect); Mark Cremer (Project Manager); Graeme Williamson
Client: Jay and Ginny Fitzgerald
Contractor: Abra Construction

MIRRORS

The Hotel, Lucerne, Switzerland
Architect: Architectures Jean Nouvel
Client: Urs Karli
Project management: Daniel Laurent
Electricity contractor: Rebsamen Elektroplanung
Ventilation: Partner Plan AG
Sanitation: Kramit Sanitar AG
Façade: Emmer Pfenniger Partner AG
Heating: Martinellii & Menti AG
Colour concept: Alain Bony
Graphics: Romano Bassi

Baccarat Flagship Store, Paris, France
Design concept: Philippe Starck
Project team: Dorothée Boissier, Grégoire Maisondieu, Astrid Courtois, Maud Bury
Project architect: José-Louis Albertini in collaboration with Hervé Jaillet
Client: Baccarat
Project team: Renaud Bereski, Ammanuel Cencig, Alphonse Goberville, Christophe Schott, Claude Vozelle, Jean-Claude Weinacker
Graphics concept: Thibaut Mathieu for Cake Design
Glass blowers: Michel Barge, Daniel Denain
Glass manufacturer/moulder: Serge Vanesson
Furniture suppliers: Atelier Thierry Goux, Droog Design, Drucker, Emeco, ENP, Gaétan Lanzani, Kettal, Laval, Orssi Angelo, Style et Confort, Techniques Transparents
Woodwork: Siam Agencement
Mirrors: Mirostyle SARL
Wallpaper: Kvadrat; Lelièvre, Pierre Frey
Tapestries: Polybe, Mallet
Floors: SMD
Carpets: Tisca France
Luminous Carpets: Fenaux Createx
Tablecloth in the Cristal Room: Porthault
Stucco: L'Atelier Blanch'art
Decorative paintings: Gilles Plagnet
Bronzes: Lambert
Sculptures: Ion Condiescu
Video and audio: SES Giraudon
Lighting concept: Voyons Voir
Lighting manufacturer: L'Atlier Fechoz
Aquarium: Coutant
Fireplaces: Bloch

New York Stock Exchange, Advanced Trading Floor, New York, USA
Architect: Asymptote
Project team: Hani Rashid, Lise Anne Couture (Principals); John Cleater, Elaine Didyk, Samuel Hassler, Sabine Muller, Folker Kleinekort, Marcos Velasques, Kevin Estrada, Henning Meyer, Carlos Ballestri
Client: New York Stock Exchange
Contractor: Morse Diesel International
Lighting design: L'Observatoire
Structural engineer: HLW International
Fabrication: Milgo Bufkin Inc

DISGUISES

Nigel Coates' Apartment, London, UK
Design and Client: Nigel Coates

Palladio Exhibition, Saló del Tinell 1996, Barcelona, Spain
Architect: BOPBAA
Project team: Josep Bohigas, Francesc Pla, Iñaki Baquero

Client: Mereo Garbin
Construction: Salvador Garcia
Collaboration: Noemí, Luca Lescio, iGuzzini, Josep Ma Rovira

Tree House, Addis Ababa, Ethiopia
Architect: Ahadu Abaineh
Local craftspeople and builders

PICTURES

My Own Room Divided, Travelling Installation, Milan, Italy
Installation concept: Nicola Pellegrini

MPV Nightclub, Leeds, UK
Architect: Union North
Project team: Miles Falkingham, David Kells
Client: MPV Ltd
Main contractor: Simons Construction Ltd
Structural engineers: Buro Happold
Joinery: Simons Joinery
Bar joinery: H & J Forbes Ltd
Electrical installation: Baseline Electrical Engineers Ltd
Glassfibre door shells and nosepieces: IJF Developments Ltd
Plumbing and sanitary; mechanical ventilation: Dawnvale Catering Equipment Specialists
Sprayed foam installation: Websters Insulation Ltd
Glazing: JMW (Aluminium) Ltd
Steel fabricator: Merseyside Ship Repairers Ltd
Painting: E & P Coatings; Bagnalls Painting and Decorating
Mastic sealant: Fastglobe (Mastics) Ltd
Sound system: 52nd Street
Security system: TI Security Ltd

Voyage Flagship Store, London, UK
Architect: Blacksheepcreatives
Project team: Joanna Sampson, Tim Nutton, Michael Delaney
Client: Tatum and Rocky Mazzilli
Contractor: Talina Builders
Structural engineer: Fluid
Stone flooring: Trinacria
Ceiling track: Harkness Hall

NESTS

Soho House Hotel, New York, USA
Creative Director: Ilse Crawford
Project team: Sue Parker (Senior Designer); Many Lax (Project Manager)
Architects: Harman Lee Jablin
Client: Soho House New York LLC
Structural engineer: James Ruderman Offices LLP

Kelly Bag Installation for Hermès Store, Barcelona, Spain
Architect: BOPBAA
Project team: Josep Bohigas, Francesc Pla, Iñaki Baquero
Client: Hermès Iberica
Audiovisual production: Zahi Shalem
Soundtrack: Jordi Dalmau
Graphic design: Marta Llinas

BasketBar, University of Utrecht, The Netherlands
Architect: NL Architects
Project team: Pieter Bannenberg, Walter van Dijk, Kamiel Klaasse, Mark Linnemann.
Collaborators: Caro Baumann, Sybran Hoek, Kirsten Huesig, Nataly Lavi, Friso Leeflang, Jennifer Petersen, Misa Shibukawa, Rolf Touzimsky, Richard Woditsch
Interior design: Nookshop Broese: Henry Betting

Interior design BasketBar (or Grand Café 'The Basket'): De Drie Musketiers
Client: Universiteit Utrecht Huisvesting
Landscape architect: NL Architects with West 8
Structural engineers: Adviesbureau voor Bouwtechniek bv; ABT Velp/Rob Nijsse
Mechanical engineers: Ingenieursburo Linssen bv
Building management: Berenschot Osborne
Contractors: Bouwbedrijf Van de Hengel bv
Installations: Van Losser bv

EGGS

The Stone House, Interpolis Headquarters, Tilburg, The Netherlands
Interior design: Marcel Wanders Studio
Architect: Bonnema Architecten
Interior architect: Nel Verschuuren of Kho Liang Le Associates
Client: Interpolis
Working ergonomics: Veldoen & Company

Sketch, London, UK
Design concept: Mourad Mazouz, Noé Duchaufour-Lawrence
Client: Mourad Mazouz
Parlour furniture: Jurgen Bey
Interior of the Lecture Room: Gabhan O'Keeffe
Interior of the Library toilets: Mehbs Yaqub
Crystals in bathrooms, curtains in the Library and Lecture Room: Swarowski
Soup trolleys: Marc Newson
Sculptures in entrance hall and West Bar: Vincent Leroy
Chandelier in East Bar: Marc Newson
Sculptural desk in lobby: Ron Arad
Invisible sculpture on stairs and laser lights in West Bar: Chris Levine

Selfridges Foodhall, Manchester, UK
Architect: Future Systems
Client: Selfridges & Co
Contractor: Interior PLC
Engineering: Arup Associates
Quantity surveyor and project management: Hanscomb

STREAMS

Karim Rashid's Apartment, New York, USA
Interior design and all furnishings: Karim Rashid
Artwork: Megan Lang; Christopher Wool
Refrigerator/dishwasher/stereo: Vintage Bang and Oulfsen
Ceramics: Ettore Sottsass, Gaetano Pesce, Matteo Thun

Ashlee House Hostel, London, UK
Architect: 24H Architecture
Project team: Maartje Lammers, Boris Zeisser
Client: Ashlee House
Builders: Bart Cuppens, Olav Bruin
Furniture: 24H projects, Maartje Lammers, Boris Zeisser constructed by Quint, Maasland

Issey Miyake Store and Headquarters, New York, USA
Architect (Sculpture): Frank O. Gehry
Architect: G TECTS LLC
Project team: Gordon Kipping (Principal); Lissa Parrott (Project Architect); Taylor Hsiao (Project Architect/sculpture); Bryan Bullen, Monica Tiulescu, Yu Duk So, Shirley Ting
Client: Issey Miyake USA Corporation
Contractor: Shimizu America Corporation
Sculpture fabricator: A. Zahner Company
Fixtures and furnishings fabricator: Atlas Industries D/F Corp.
Mural artist: Alejandro Gehry
Structural engineers: Gilsanz Murray Steficek LLP

Mechanical, electrical, plumbing, fire safety engineers: Marino Gerazounis &
Jaffe Associates, LLC
Lighting designer: L'Observatoire International Lighting Designers and
Consultants
Elevator consultant: Van Deusen Associates
Building & zoning law consultants: William Vitacco Associates Ltd
Preservation consultant: Integrated Conservation Resources, Inc
Landmarks consultant: Higgins & Quasebarth
Specification consultant: Construction Specifications, Inc

RIBBONS

Claydon Heeley Jones Mason Advertising Agency, London, UK
Architect: Ushida Findlay
Project team: Kathryn Findlay (Director in Charge); Peter Maxwell (Project
Architect)
Client: Claydon Heeley Jones Mason
Main contractor: Interior plc (special works department)
Service engineer: Fulcrum Consulting
Quantity surveyor: Mike Porter Associates
Acoustical consultant: Fulcrum Consulting
Audiovisual consultant: Wave Ltd

L'Una Hotel Vittoria, Florence, Italy
Architect: Fabio Novembre
Project team: Carlo Formisano, Lorenzo de Nicola, Giuseppina Flor, Ramon
Karges
Client: UNA Hotels and Resorts
Main contractor: Tino Sana srl
General contractor: C.P.F
Electricity: Consorzio Artim
Air conditioning: Gino Battaglini
Hall:
Floor covering: Pastellone Veneziano by Collezioni Ricordi
Special structures: Loop by Tino Sana covered with Opus Romano by
Bisazza
Lighting: Modular, chandelier by Nucleo
Seating: AND sofa by Fabio Novembre for Cappellini
Restaurant:
Floor covering: Opus Romano by Bisazza
Wall covering: MDF by Marotte
Special structures: Tino Sano (tables); Zella (stained glass)
Lighting: iGuzzini
Furniture: Lensvelt
Conference Room:
Special structures: curved wall by Tino Sana
Lighting: Modular, RGB System by Zumtobel
Furniture: Fritz Hansen
Rooms:
Floor coverings: Tino Sana, laminate by Locatelli, mosaic by Bisazza
Wall coverings: leather by Cuoium
Lighting: iGuzzini; fibre optics by Fort Fibre Ottiche
Furniture: La Palma and Cappellini
Corridors:
Floor covering: gress by Cotto d'Este
Wall covering: laminate by Locatelli
Special structures: MDF shapes and frames by Tino Sana
Lighting: Modular, iGuzzini

Emporio Armani, Chater Road, Hong Kong
Architect: Massimiliano and Doriana Fuksas
Project team: Davide Stolfi (Project Leader); Iain Wadham, Defne Dilber,
Motohiro Takada (design team); Gianluca Brancaleone, Nicola Cabiati, Andrea
Marazzi (model makers)
Client: Giorgio Armani
Floor: Sikafloor, Germany
Furniture: Massimiliano and Doriana Fuksas, manufactured by Zeus Noto

Glass showcases: Sunglass
Lights: iGuzzini
Vases in Armani Fiori: Monte di Rovello
Façade signage: Nettuno Neon

CLOUDS

Wave UFO, Travelling Installation
First installed at Kunsthaus, Bregenz, Austria and then at 590 Madison
Avenue, New York
Design concept: Mariko Mori

Blur Building, Part of the Arteplage Yverdon-les-Bains Installation for
Swiss Expo 2002, Biel, Switzerland.
Architect: Diller + Scofidio
Project team: Elizabeth Diller, Ricardo Scofidio (Principals); Dirk Hebel
(Project Leader); Charles Renfro, Eric Bunge
Client: EXPO 02 by extasia
Structural engineers: Passera & Pedretti
Sound installation: Christian Marclay
Media: Diller + Scofidio in collaboration with Ben Rubin of EAR Studio
Media associate: Mark Wasiuta

Bloomberg Ice, Tokyo, Japan
Architect: Klein Dytham Architecture
Project team: Mark Dytham, Astric Klein (Principals); Yoshinori Nishimura,
Keisuke Inatsugu, Chika Muto
Client: Bloomberg L.P.
Media artist: Toshio Iwai
Project management: Bovis Lend Lease
Contractor: D. Brain
LED manufacturer: Starlet Furniture: Interoffice

MOVIES

FluxSpace 3.0-Mscape Installation for Documenta XI, 2002, Kassel,
Germany
Architect: Asymptote.
Project team: Hani Rashid, Lise Anne Couture (Principals), Noboru Ota, John
Cleater

D-Edge Nightclub, São Paulo, Brazil
Architect: Muti Randolph
Project team: Muti Randolph, Carol Bueno, Paulo Filisetti
Client: Renato Ratier
General contractor: Triptyque
Lighting manufacturers: New Light (neon); ICB (LED's equaliser); Lundardi
(dmx)
Wood furniture: Silvestre de Oliveira
Wall cushion: Claudio Alves
Glasses: Geraldo Cruz
Mason: Gilberto dos Santos
Poliuretanic resin: Adriana Addam

Shell Electric Storm Installation, South Bank, London, UK
Design concept: Shell in collaboration with The Renewable Energy Systems
(RES), part of the Sir Robert McAlpine Group
Sponsorship: The Department of Trade and Industry, Fortis Bank, EDF Energy
and international law firm, Norton Rose
Wind turbine: Vestas
Sound system: Timax

INDEX

Acknowledgements

The publishers would like to thank the following for permission to reproduce the images in this book. While they have made every effort to trace copyright holders they would be pleased, if informed, to correct any errors or omissions in subsequent editions of this publication.

Courtesy Ahadu Abaineh (21 inset, 87 inset, 114–117); Courtesy Ashlee House (160–161); Courtesy Atelier van Lieshout (82–85, 199 inset); Courtesy Asymptote (190–193); Luc Boegly (20 inset, 98–101, 127 inset); Joseph Burn (12 inset, 38–41, 46–49, 120 inset); Leon Chew (42 inset, 90–93); David Churchill (166–169); Etienne Clement (34–37, 172 inset); Courtesy of André and Coqueline Courreges (66–69, 167 inset); Richard Davies (67 inset, 150–153); Courtesy Dia Center for the Arts (54 inset, 55 inset, 61–65, 89 inset); Courtesy Diller + Scofidio (182–185, 201 inset); Bernd Druffel (54–55, 188 inset); Courtesy El Ultimo Grito (58–61, 193); Alberto Ferrero (30–33, 69 inset, 95 inset, 143 inset, 157 inset, 170–173); Rômulo Fialdini (2, 53 inset, 194–197); Jean Francois Jaussad/ luxproduction (154–157); David Joseph/SNAPS (50–53, 183 inset, 194 inset); Katsuhisa Kida (103 inset, 125 inset, 139 inset, 187, 188–189); John Keenan (61 inset, 77 inset, 122–125); Luuk Kramer (138 left and middle); Carlo Lavatori (70–73, 85 inset, 200 inset); André Lichtenberg (17–21, 49 inset, 189 inset); Raf Makda/VIEW (44 right, 45 right); Courtesy NL Architects (55–57); Ottonella Mocellin (56 inset, 120–121); Nacasa & Partners (4, 26–29, 41 inset, 78–81, 105 inset, 153 inset, 157 inset, 176 inset); NYSE/SIAC/Asymptote (71 inset, 102–105, 175 inset); Frank Oudeman (162–165, 174 inset); Oscar Paisley (42); Giorgio Possenti (101 inset, 106–109, 133 inset); Courtesy Public Art Fund, New York: Tom Powell Imaging (25 inset, 144 inset, 159 inset, 178–181, inset); Prat Ramon (66 inset, 140 inset, 169 inset, 174–177); Julia Rhodes RES (201 right); Christian Richters (10–13, 107 inset, 128 inset, 135 inset, 158–159); Martyn Rose (131 inset, 146–149, 189 inset); Philippe Ruault (18 inset, 27 inset, 94–97, 147 inset, 185 inset); Eva Serrats (36 inset, 110–113, 113 inset, 134–137, 163 inset, 197 inset, 199 inset); Courtesy Shell Electric Storm (99 inset, 183 inset, 198–201 left); Edmund Summers (81 inset, 126–129, 133 inset, 165 inset); Jan Takagi (57 inset, 186 left); Martyn Thompson (40 inset, 58 inset 117 inset, 130–133, 158 inset, 161 inset); Marco Vaglieri (118–120); Hans Van Leeuwen (17 inset, 139 right, 140–141, 177 inset); Hein van Liempd (14–17, 123 inset); Frederik Vercruysee (86–89, 111 inset, 141 inset); Morely von Sternberg (37 inset, 43, 44 left, 45 middle 90 inset); Courtesy Marcel Wanders Studio (29 inset, 64 inset, 142–145, 181 inset); Paul Warchol (22–25, 74–77, 88 inset, 150 inset).

Vertical Inserts – as above, plus :-

Luc Boegly (126); Courtesy Dia Foundation (8); Alberto Ferrero (8, 143, 156); David Joseph/SNAPS (2–3); Katsuhisa Kida (184); John Keenan (121); André Lichtenberg (69, 188); Nacasa and Partners (8), Giorgio Possenti (148); Christian Richters (10–11); Eva Serrats (152, 194); Martyn Thompson (116); Hans Van Leeuwen (83); Frederik Vercruysee (112)